PATRIMONIES

PATRIMONIES

Short Stories by
R.V. CASSILL

&
Ampersand Press
Creative Writing Program
Roger Williams College
Bristol, RI 02809

Acknowledgment is made to the following publications in which these stories previously appeared:

Esquire: "The Father"

Jeopardy: "The Gadfly"

University of Kansas City Review: "Hatcher's Devil"

New American Review No. 3: "The Rationing of Love"

Perspective: "The Prize"

"In the Central Blue" first appeared in *Man and the Movies,* Louisiana State University Press, and is reprinted in *Writing Fiction,* Prentice-Hall.

"The Prize" was reprinted in *Prize Stories 1956, The O'Henry Awards,* and "Hatcher's Devil" was reprinted in *Best Articles and Stories, 1956,* Indiana University Press.

Library of Congress Catalog Card Number: 87-72427
ISBN 0-935331-05-0

Cover photo by Kay Cassill
Composition by NewPaper Graphics
131 Washington St.
Providence, RI 02903
Layout and design by NewPaper Graphics and Ampersand Press
Printed in U.S.A.

Published by Ampersand Press, Creative Writing Program, Roger Williams College, Bristol, RI 02809

This book is for Orin and Jesse Cassill
and for
William and William Verlin Wood

This is my son, my own Telemachus,
To whom I leave the sceptre and the isle—
Tenneyson—*Ulysses*

CONTENTS

The Prize

The first prize in the contest sponsored by the Goodyear Tire Company early in the Depression was, I remember, an overwhelmingly large one. It was probably $25,000; at any rate it was a sum on that scale, one large enough to inspire a variety of religious experience among contestants, and the scattering of lesser prizes had been conceived with similar grandeur. Looking back from a removal of two decades and from some comprehension of the economic and political turns of those years I am impelled to visualize the Goodyear Co. struggling with titanic anxiety to shake free of the chaos that threatened organizations as well as individuals, and willy-nilly I have to admire the scale of their effort. They knew how big a battle we were in.

And I remember with a twinge that at the time of the contest I didn't even know there was a Depression. I knew we had moved out of the city to live near Chesterfield—where my father was to work in his cousin's grain elevator—for reasons that were not very happy or decent. But it seemed to me when I weighed everything that we had been expelled because of something ugly or shameful that my family had done or because of some shameful inadequacy in us into which it was best not to inquire too far. When I learned, from eavesdropping on adult conversation, that my father had lost $380 in a bank failure, I was ashamed of him for not having had more on deposit. We lost our car then, too, and I was pretty sure that this need not have happened if he had had more of the installments paid on it.

There was very little talk between my parents which named the name of Depression. Since they were both faithful Republicans who supported Hoover to the end, it might well have seemed traitorous to them to use such a term—I figured then it was like *not* holding your breath when something very important depended on your holding it.

A big green van took our furniture to the house near Chesterfield, and the family followed in the car borrowed from my father's cousin. We arrived on a rainy evening just before dark, and there was the van backed up to the house with the moving men carrying our familiar things into its dark interior. Our rocking chairs, the fernery, and the radio were going in where they didn't belong. The thought struck me that we were moving into a house that no one lived in. That was so strange. And whatever mystery was being enacted, I didn't want it to happen. I wanted to hold my breath long enough to keep it from happening.

Through the rainy fall of our first year in Chesterfield, while I was trying to get used to the tiny school, to the overpowering skills of the farm boys who were my new classmates, and to the big old house we now lived in, I concentrated fiercely and stupidly on the problem of our expulsion from the city and began to see it as an omen of a world committed totally to sorrow. I learned to read the most trivial disappointments as signs that the race itself was doomed.

Walking home after school between the cornfields that bordered the road I would hear the brittle noise of rain on the cornleaves and the surliness inside me would cry back to it, "Yes, that's the way things are, all right." In the dripping of the rain from the porch roof outside my window I saw a melting of even my memories of the time when things had been fun, and whatever I found disheartening or miserable I cherished.

Separating myself more than formerly from my brothers, who were two and three years older than I, I cultivated an almost erotic pursuit of tokens of decay. In this I was aided by one of the rooms on the second floor that had served all the former tenants in lieu of an attic.

Books, old magazines, a sewing machine, dress forms, and trunks of·many funny sorts were piled in this room. Probably there was some sort of stipulation in the rental agreement that we were to have only "the rest" of the house, for my brothers and I had been forbidden to play in there. But if I was quiet I could slip into it from my own room without my mother's hearing me where she worked in the downstairs kitchen.

In the room a smell of paper decomposing welcomed me and alerted my senses to a kind of dream that was detailed by the thousand articles of use and the souvenirs I stirred out of the trunks. I found an old cane with a metal bust of Lincoln for its head, the metal bearing an inscription linking it to the Republican convention of 1884. One of the trunks was half full of arrowheads and stone knives, some of them bearing paper tags that indicated they had been found in the river bluffs east of town. There was a stack of tintypes in another trunk which included pictures of the depot and the dedication of the Methodist Church. (If I wanted to I could look up and see this church through the window, sitting shabbily at the edge of a cornfield, now arched over with the elms that appeared in the tintype as twigs stuck in the loam around it. As far as one could see in such views the half-lumnious white of ripe corn floored the river valley. I'd heard my father say in one of his moments of optimism that this was the richest soil on earth except for the Nile valley, and I worked on this idea too, converting it so I could gloat on these riches strung senselessly under the rains and consoling my bitterness by noting how universal the waste of things was.)

A green trunk in that room yielded a box of nickled instruments which I now realize were the old-fashioned paraphernalia of a woman's douche, and which had for me then, ignorant as I was of their function, some quality of terminated ferocity, like the arrowheads piled in the trunk bottom—no longer an arsenal, but something oddly more than a mass of junk.

When my mother found out that I had been playing in the forbidden room and asked what right I had to be there, I told her I had been reading the old magazines and books—which was not untrue. I didn't tell her that I had jimmied the locks on most of the trunks or that I had read batches of the old letters I found in them. Anyway, she discovered more trespasses by finding some of the arrowheads in the treasure box that I kept in one of my drawers and by noting small bits of vandalism. I had broken the head of Lincoln from the cane and for no good reason (except to mock at earthly vanity) had rubbed its nose off on the sharp edge of a lock.

She came after me with some determination then. She really insisted on an explanation of why I liked that room well enough to play there so much. "With that dirty old stuff," she said.

"Like with the arrowheads," I told her solemnly, "it would help me remember there used to be Indians right around here in the olden times."

"Ah," she said, mildly impressed and placated. "I see. With them you could sort of pretend that the Indians were still alive and more real. I see. Then I suppose you could understand your history better and the way things are by using that Republican cane."

She looked at me sharply. "Why did you break the cane then?"

"I don't know."

"You shouldn't have done that to Lincoln. He was such a great man," she said with a faraway look that seemed to suggest he should have been my father. "It was awfully wrong to break him up like that, but I'm glad if otherwise you learned anything."

My pretended agreement with her was a great fraud because her optimistic interpretation was so exactly wrong in its tendency. It had not been any sense of life in these trinkets that excited me. As they went through my hands I had exulted in them because they were evidence that so many who had been alive were dead and gone.

Far as she was from appreciating the content of my play in the closed room, my mother must have worried about it and found it inadequate, as she found so many things in our life at Chesterfield inadequate.

She had a bundle of grievances, and I think sometimes that what carried us through that winter and marked all of us forever with a special stamp was her refusal to admit the slipping downward that obviously accompanied our move to the little town. She had to take it, but she wouldn't have it. She was going to lure me out of the old storeroom into some healthy activity whatever the cost, and for a while there was talk of getting me a subscription to the *Youth's Companion*, even if that meant showing favoritism to me, since nothing comparable could be afforded "just then" for the older boys.

With the same frustrated force she approached the problem of utilities. There was no electricity in Chesterfield then and no bathroom in our house. From our arrival on she set the resources of her anguish to work on getting us a Delco light plant and plumbing, though with all her emotional heave in this direction and her heckling of my father she never worked out a practical plan by which we might expect to have them. She merely made us all hate fetching water from the pump more than we might have otherwise and made us all feel we would go stone blind from reading by a kerosene lamp.

What she couldn't hold on to with a full grasp she meant to cling to, as long as necessary, with her fingernails, and the obvious pity of this was that she could get her nails into nothing solid except us.

It was her passion's refusal to admit that things had changed which swept us into the Goodyear contest with such velocity and finally made it intolerable not to win.

Winter had come by the time the contest was announced. The evening we heard of it my brother George and I were in the kitchen helping my mother with the dishes while my father and older brother listened to the radio in the dining room.

"Hear that?" my mother cried out all at once. I thought she'd at least heard a car stopping at our front gate. But she motioned us to be still, and we got most of the announcement, not quite all. She marched into the dining room and demanded that my father explain the details she had missed.

"I wasn't entirely listening," he said guiltily, sleepily. "Just enjoying what they had to say."

"Enjoying? I don't see what there is to *enjoy* when he's talking about a contest. You ought to be listening attentively, or I don't know what's the point of listening at all."

"I know," he agreed. "I'll tell you what. It sounded like someone was going to get a patch of money, all right. I did hear them say there was a first prize of twenty-five thousand dollars. Moreover there's a whole kaboodle of little prizes."

"Little?" my mother wailed indignantly. "Why—why—*little!* I heard myself that there were thousand-dollar prizes."

"I meant even smaller ones. Little dee-rigibles and things."

"A thousand dollars." My mother mourned his unconcern for this. "That's not so much it would wear our brains out figuring what to do with it. I wish you'd listen at the end of the program and be sure to get the details down on a piece of paper. No. You call me in if there's any more going to be said about it."

He took off his glasses and polished them slowly. "You sit down here and listen, Mother. The boys and I can finish the dishes. You're quicker at these things than I am."

"All I asked was for you to call me. Can't you even do that?" my mother demanded. "I know you're tired from your work and I wouldn't ask any more of you today."

Since he was in our big rocker and sitting as relaxed as a man can

15

get and since it obviously wouldn't be much trouble for him to listen to the announcement, he naturally took her comment as sarcasm. So, when she'd gone back to her work, he tuned in another program.

"You hear that, Mama?" George said, wiping away like a good fellow at the dishes. "He's turned it off."

"Well," she said, "he's tired and cranky. He worked awfully hard today. You know it's hard work at the elevator."

Then my father appeared at the kitchen door. In those days he was still wearing some of his old business suits to work, and they always had grain dust in their fibers no matter how well he brushed them when he came home. The whitish dust in his clothes gave him an air of being faded like a picture from which some of the ink has been rubbed. He made a curious gesture, half in anger, half in appeasement, like a doubter crossing himself.

"You know what these darn contests are, Sally," he pleaded. "They don't mean anyone any good. They're only done to advertise the product."

"We'll talk about it later," my mother said. This was recognized by all as a threat.

"Did you personally ever know anyone who had won his postage back in a contest like that?"

"We'll not discuss it until the boys are asleep," she warned him. I think he began making up his mind to submit right then. I saw him swallow and then nod reassurance to himself that it might not be as bad as he feared it could be.

From that first evening on, for weeks, our family had the contest like a vocation or a disease. Of course it was easy enough for my mother to find out the details of competition once she had made up our minds, and by the end of the week she and each of us boys were working on our individual lists of words that could be made from the letters comprised in the name GOODYEAR TIRE AND RUBBER COMPANY. That was the task of the contest.

You can see that the first words come easily: dog, god, ray, rite, and so on. It is when these are all put down that the game becomes tantalizing and demoralizing. Then the tongue tries nonsense syllables and combinations in the hope that some lightly hidden word will fall out to be added to the list. And that makes quite a noise in the house.

Once at supper I began mumbling to myself, and my father, driven beyond exasperation, slammed down his water glass and howled, "Groggy wayorv, boogly, boogly, woogly, arf." Then he glared around the table with the tears of the rejected squeezing angrily out of the corners of his eyes.

"Not at the table," my mother cautioned me. She turned to my father. "I don't know why you're so set against what the boys are ambitious enough to try to do. I should think you might better want to help them."

"I won't. Great Jesus, I won't," he said helplessly. "What in His name would I be helping them to do? Lose their minds and jabber like apes?"

"They've been working with our dictionary, and I don't know that *that's* bad for their education," my mother said. "The contest gives them something to look forward to." She satisfied herself with such explanations, and for my part I was thinking self-righteously that my father, in his outburst, had used *f* and *v*, which, of course, were not permissible under the laws of the game.

According to my mother's first, rather easygoing plan, each of us was to work exclusively on his own list and even keep it partly secret from the others so there would be a sort of intra-family contest as well as the larger one. We worked from the dictionary by turns. It seemed to me sometimes when I was blundering unsystematically through it, dreaming by lamplight, that each of us might win a prize that suited his own intelligence and deserts. My mother would probably get one of the thousand-dollar prizes. Dave and George might or might not get something. Maybe one of them would get a fifty-dollar prize, since they were older than I. For myself, I thought and felt that I should win one of the chrome-plated models of the dirigible *Akron*, the lowest prize offered. I think probably a hundred of these models were being given away. I remember telling my mother that I didn't think I was good enough to win more than a model, but that this suited me because I would rather have it than money anyhow. Altogether I managed to make this model into an image of what I was worth and of what the world would pay me for being what I was.

"You have to work hard if that's the prize you want," my mother warned. "Don't forget there'll be people from all over the country trying to win, just like you are."

When the deadline for submitting entries was approaching, my mother decided that we needed a larger dictionary to work from and that we should borrow one from the school. The question of who should borrow it became major. One of us boys should ask our teacher, she thought, but we all balked at this as being too embarrassing. The other boys got away with this argument, but I was caught—perhaps because I had done more excited talking about the contest than they.

"There's nothing wicked about borrowing a dictionary," my mother bullied me. "We're not doing something dishonest. We're working as hard as we know how to earn something, and if more people would do that I expect our country would be better off. Just explain to your teacher...."

This is odd, but maybe if I had believed that we were in the contest for the sake of competition, I wouldn't have minded explaining to my teacher why I wanted the dictionary. Caught as I was in the dream of certainly winning a thousand dollars and a dirigible, I couldn't face it. It seemed to me like putting on airs to go to my teacher and admit the glory my family was headed for.

So my mother finally borrowed it. I remember her coming in through the snowy yard, a little after I had come home from school, with the big dictionary wrapped in a shawl to protect it from the mist in the air. Her face before she saw me was set with a harsh intensity, as of someone who has refused humiliation by sheer refusal to recognize it. Seeing me, she smiled and said, "Look. I borrowed it from your teacher after you'd left. She was good about lending it. Now you see that she would have lent it to you if you'd only asked her. Don't you see?"

"But what's she going to think of us?" After all, it was I who had to go to school the next day and possibly face my teacher's amusement, envy, or scorn.

"I didn't tell her what we were using it for," my mother said with a sly grimace that she meant to be comforting. "I fibbed to her, so don't you worry."

When I thought this over I announced that I didn't want to do the contest any more. My mother flung her arms around me and pressed my face very hard against her side. "Of course you do," she said. "We've worked so doggone hard this far that I'm convinced we're going to win. Maybe not the grand prize, but something. There's no reason why you can't win that dirigible if you want it. Don't you see that yet?" She frightened me with her determination, and even that was a lesser thing than the sheer giant onrush of the contest, beginning to reveal its true scope.

In the last week before the deadline—and this must have been in late January, at about the time of the thaws, when the three of us boys would have liked to be playing outside—my mother bore down on us all. Some one of us had to be at the dictionary all the time. There wasn't any more talk of the contest's being educational or fun. It was work and we had to work hard enough to win. We combined our lists now, at least to the extent that our inefficient systems permitted. We had begun without much system at all,

boys would have liked to be playing outside—my mother bore down on us all. Some one of us had to be at the dictionary all the time. There wasn't any more talk of the contest's being educational or fun. It was work and we had to work hard enough to win. We combined our lists now, at least to the extent that our inefficient systems permitted. We had begun without much system at all, and, except for my mother's, our penmanship was terrible. So whether a word discovered in the dictionary at this late date or on someone else's list could legitimately be added to ours was a matter none of us could be quite sure of. Certainly each of us had duplications in his list, and none of us ever had quite the same total as any of the others, though we tried to balance them for a while. Very late my mother tried to get us to alphabetize our lists, but this only got us in more tangles.

On the last afternoon Dave went to the post office immediately after school with his list and George's—that was a nervous precaution, since they had to be postmarked that day and some act of God might demolish the post office or block the road to it if we waited until too late.

On the other two lists, at my mother's insistence, we were adding all kinds of the nonsense combinations which earlier had been only a means of helping us find pure words. Some of these, she said, we might have missed in the dictionary, and it was the responsibility of the judges to decide if they were eligible or not. "*Reay*," she said. "That could be a girl's name. Put it down anyway. *Burrec*. That sounds like a kind of donkey, I guess. *Yarg*. I don't see why that shouldn't be a word if there's a word *yard*. One doesn't sound like it meant any more than the other one, does it?"

She had the clock sitting on the table where we worked—the post office closed at six—and I knew that now nothing but time running out would stop her. My father came into this intensity and stood behind us, watching us without saying anything. Pretty soon my mother spoke over her shoulder to him. "If you're not going to help, go somewhere else. Go start the fire in the kitchen. I'll get supper as soon as we're finished."

"I won't," he said. And then, after a long deliberation, "God

19

damn the Goodyear Tire and Rubber Corporation."

"Company," I said.

"I suppose you mean God damn me," my mother said.

"I don't," he said. "I mean—"

"Shoo. Go on. I can't think while you're staring at me."

He went into the bedroom and after some banging of dresser drawers returned to throw an envelope and two ten-dollar bills on the list of words she was working on. "There," he said in a tone that was dignified only by its slightness. "There's some money and my insurance policy. I'm leaving."

"Ha," my mother said.

"You've turned the boys against me and driven them half crazy with this contest. I warned you not to do it."

"Then leave," my mother said. "*Dooger.*"

After he was gone she kept muttering more and more absurd combinations of syllables. Her face flamed, and I could see a vein in her temple bulge with effort, but she was not writing down any more of her inventions.

She looked up at George long enough to say, "Follow him and see where he goes." Then she glanced hard at the clock and told me to get my coat and rubbers and be ready to run for the post office. "We can't be late," she said. "You can run part of the way or go Scout's pace. You know how to do that."

With an attempt to cheer me, she said, "You and I have more words than the others now."

But, giving a last look at the physical ugliness of my list, I said I wished there were time to copy at least this afternoon's work.

"Maybe if they can't quite make out some of them that will be a good thing," she said craftily. Her imagination apparently had strained to cover every accident of incompetence, weakness, taste, or unfairness on the part of the unknown judges, and it seemed to me that she had intended that each of our lists be somehow corrupt to fit the imagined corruptness of the major human types.

As I was going out with the big manila envelopes containing our two lists, George arrived back to report that my father had started west across the cornfield, had cut back within about a quarter of a mile, climbed the fence into the road, and was right now hiding inside a culvert about two hundred yards from the house.

"Ha," my mother said. Her voice crackled with unhappy triumph. "I supposed he wouldn't go far. He'll get hungry after a little while and come in. Now *run*," she commanded me. "Be sure you make it to the post office."

20

The culvert where my father was hiding was an obstacle in the road now. I could hardly bring myself to walk over him like that, but I knew I had to hurry. The road was wet. Now at sundown it was beginning to freeze, and I could feel the delicate ice crunch under every step with a beautiful sound and sensation of touch. The rosy light over the cornfield, reflected in a thousand puddles islanded in the loam, seemed to me too strongly and unhappily beautiful for me to stand, and it occurred to me that I might die right then, being so divided by feelings I had never encountered before, weakening to my first realization that living was something that one must choose against hardship to do.

At the culvert I left the road, knelt in the water of the ditch bottom and looked in at my father. He was sitting right in the middle of the concrete tube. In the dim light I could only see his silhouette and the glitter of reflected light in his eyes. I am sure he saw me, but neither of us spoke.

Then I ran for the post office. I think I ran all the way, because I got there in plenty of time to put the envelopes in the letter box. Walking home afterward I felt how my knees were wet from where I had knelt in the ditch.

Of course none of us won anything from the Goodyear Co. In about a month the winners of prizes over a thousand dollars were announced. First prize went to someone who had over three times as many words in his list as there had been in the largest of ours.

"Three times," my mother said. "That's a lie. That can't be. They must have used foreign words like French and German, Spanish and all. And they *said* that was against the rules."

My father commented, "Maybe one of you will win a littler prize. They're going to announce more next week." After the bad day of the mailing of the lists he had relaxed, had been permitted to relax, and by this time was even displaying a mild hope that something might come from all that bother.

But then the last of the cash prizes was announced and there was nothing left to wait for except the names of the winners of the model dirigibles.

"If the others didn't get any money I'm not going to win the dirigible," I said to my father, answering one of his soft optimisms aggressively.

"You don't know," he said. "I wouldn't wonder that your list would be just right for a smaller prize. You know, it might be like

21

having the right tool for the right job."

"Yes, the right tool," my mother said. "We should have had a typewriter. I can understand that now that it's too late. Even if they didn't specify that you had to use a typewriter."

"You told me that my words they couldn't read might be a good thing," I said.

"Well, on that...." Her lips worked carefully while she made up her mind how to answer me. "Yes, that may be so. Don't give up hope."

From this last posture she established against defeat and from my own premonitory sense of loss I began to develop the notion that they were all *demanding* that I win, and I added the strain of what I considered their expectations to my own. Partly for them, partly for myself I strained all the tricks of emotional force—on the order of holding my breath, crossing my fingers, figuratively—to affect what the announcer was going to say when he came to read the last list of winners. I accepted, in a subterranean agreement, that I owed it to the family to win, for if I won that would help make up for my father's hiding in the culvert, my mother's fibbing to the teacher, and our general humiliation in prostrating ourselves before a big company that had so far ignored us.

Each name on that list of winners should have been mine, and none was. I wanted to howl when the reading was over, and yet I felt that, having lost, I didn't even have the right to do that. For the first time it came to me with undeniable force that beyond our mere failure to win we had lost something that had been put at stake.

After the trial of listening my father sighed tranquilly and said it appeared to him that these last prizes had been awarded on a geographical basis. "Did you notice how there was hardly ever more than two from any state except New York? You heard how this gentleman up in Red Oak got one. Well sir, that's enough for this part of the world, they likely figured. You can't tell me these contests aren't rigged some way. Naturally you didn't have much of a chance when they did things like that," he told me.

He put out his hand to rumple my hair or pat my cheek, but I flung myself beyond his reach, behaving spitefully to cover my sense of worthlessness.

"There, there, feller," he said. "There, there, now."

"I worked hard," I screeched. "I had as good a list as anybody's."

"Sure you did. I'd lay money you had a better one than some of those as got the money."

I said, "I'm going to kill someone for this."

His head jerked as though I had burned him. Then his eyes searched beyond me for my mother, and he seemed to be crawling humbly and with awkward slowness to some complicity with her. I saw this happen, but I chose then not to understand it. I thought I understood how every man's hand was against me. From then on.

"Everything comes to he who waits," my father said. "You'll see that, because that's the way things are. You remember when we came here we had such a hard job getting along without electricity and didn't think we'd ever have any?"

He paused for me to answer and I wouldn't.

"Now they're putting a line in," he said in a hearty tone, as though I might care about *that*. "They're going to bring the wire down from Parsons to Chesterfield and we'll have it out here, too. Then we can get us an electric radio and a lot of things, maybe. They were unloading poles on the other side of Chesterfield today."

"Somebody else got my dirigible," I whined.

"It would only be a little tin thing. You couldn't have any play out of it. Your mother and I thought that when the roads dry up we'd get you a bicycle. Wouldn't you rather have that?"

I set up an awful racket, protesting that I didn't want a bicycle or anything else but the dirigible. To which my father replied that I only wanted what I couldn't have and if that was the way of it he couldn't help me. I believed this dictum, if nothing else he said. I heard it wailing through my dreams that night like a sentence of wrath to come. Maybe on purpose I dreamed toward morning that all my family was dead. My father was dead in the culvert where he had hidden, and I was kicking up wet grass from the ditch to cover him in.

At school time I pretended to be sick so I could stay home. As a matter of fact, I sulked with such ugliness that my mother suggested on her own part that I should go play in the storeroom, where I had not been for some months. I considered her recommendation and even walked upstairs to glance in at my former retreat. The dead room would not receive me, and the chilly smell of it really nauseated me. Losing the contest had even cut me off from that.

Everything was so senseless I might as well go do it like the rest until I was dead. I would just be too smart to hope for anything again, that was all.

But they tricked me back from that state too. I came from school one evening about a month later to find my model of the dirigible *Akron* on the dining room table. There was a mass of wrapping paper broken back from around it and some excelsior that smelled like newly sawed lumber.

It was a very shiny model, though somewhat smaller and harsher-looking than I had imagined it would be. It said GOODYEAR TIRE AND RUBBER CO. on the side.

"What's it for?" I yelled to my mother as she came in from the kitchen to see how I was going to receive it. "Did one of us win after all?"

She smiled her best. "Sure," she said. "Isn't it a pretty thing, now? I guess this proves that if you do your level best and really want something you'll get it, doesn't it?"

I might have accepted the moral of her comment without argument, for moral significance seemed to me at that point lighter than air, but the practical account worried me. "How come they didn't read our name on the radio if we won?"

"We didn't *exactly* win," my mother said. "Your father and I thought that you'd worked so hard that you *were* a winner and deserved a prize. We wrote to that man in Red Oak and bought it from him."

"Oh," I said. Why did they do that to me on top of all the rest? I couldn't stand it, and I said, "Thanks a lot."

Just before suppertime my brother Dave caught me outside in the yard and said, "All right, you big jackass, you got your dee-ridge-able. Aren't you proud of it?"

"You leave me alone."

"I'm going to leave you alone. They had to pay fifteen bucks for it and now maybe we can't have a bicycle this summer."

"I never asked them to do it."

"Oh, no," he said. "Oh, no, you didn't. Just whining like a pup that you didn't get anything in this contest. Did any of the rest of us get anything?"

"I didn't want them to buy it. I didn't know they'd be such big fools."

"I don't know," he said despairingly. "I guess they were because *you're* such a big fool. Listen, if you don't make them think that you're real glad to get it I'll kill you."

It was not—or not exactly—his threat that weighed on me. When he left me I had nothing to face except—as on the evening of my father's flight—the width of sundown and spring air, empty but nonetheless resonant with things learned and half-learned, again multiplying by its beauty and silence the real threat of death if I turned away from my family and their organized ways of stinging me. I could see then that I would have to keep pretending the dirigible was fine, and I have never learned what else I could have said.

In the Central Blue

Ordinarily I considered it no drawback that there was no theater in our little farming town of Chesterfield. But in the case of World War I air movies I felt different. At puberty I was very airminded, and it seemed a large disaster when I missed *Wings.*

The week it played in Nebraska City spring thaws took the bottom out of the gravel road for miles east of the bridge we would have to cross to get there. Toward the end of the week when the road began to get firmer, I was struck down by fever and diarrhea. My affliction was probably brought on by anxiety about the road conditions and by arguing with my father about whether, at full power and with three boys to push, his Essex might not churn its way through the bad spots to the bridge.

My older brother and my best friend Hudson Fowler saw the picture, driving over to Nebraska City at the week's end with a truck full of other kids from Chesterfield. From an upstairs window I watched

27

the truck pull away, crouched in my weakness, nursing the envy manifested in the uncontrollable, spastic burning of my gut. My father hunted me out to say that if I "had taken care of myself"—instead of dashing across wet lawns and fields outside of town all week without boots to prove that the earth was *not* mirey underfoot—I might now be going with the others. If I just hadn't got so excited about a darn airplane movie, I wouldn't have overtaxed my system.

The lesson was plain enough without his pointing the moral. But I wouldn't have it. In the darkness of the privy that evening I shit it away. In their wobbly, sassy little Spads, the boys had gone up there without me. The little line of dots pocked the canvas of their fuselages. Spitting black blood, their clean American faces lolled on the padded rims of the cockpits. In his black triplane with a black scarf crackling in the slipstream, the Kraut laughed at us all. Wind whistled around the ill-fitting privy door. Its mockery and the stink of my own excrement were no more offensive to me than my father's common sense judgment on my psychosomatic folly. I rebelled against them all.

So, if I had missed *Wings*, I was not going to miss *Hell's Angels*. After so long a time, I'm not sure how much later, it came to the theater in Nebraska City. It must have come at least a year afterward, because by then both my friend Hudson and I had graduated into high school, my older brother got to take the car out in the evening for dates, and I was in love with Hudson's blonde and titless cousin Betty.

I loved her ignorantly, impurely, and intermittently, sometimes unfurling toward her passions that had been cultivated for other objects and which were, no doubt, more appropriate when directed toward building model airplanes, shooting Germanic spatsies from the mulberry tree with antiaircraft fire from my Stevens' Crackshot, or working up nurse-aviator fantasies by a near simultaneous reading of *War Aces* and *Silver Screen* magazines.

Good little Betty couldn't have known what I wanted of her when I scrimmaged for a seat next to her in algebra class. At Halloween of our freshman year I caught her by accident as she was coming—costumed and masked—across the parking lot to the back entrance of the high school building to the party. She couldn't have known what I did to her then when I drew her out of the moonlight into the shadow of the fire escape and kissed her. I took off running in the direction of the Chesterfield grain elevator and went past it for a mile down the

28

moon-glinting railroad tracks, convinced that I had done to her what Lieutenant Frank Luke did to the French nurse before he took off for his last spree of balloon busting.

So she couldn't have known what I had in store for her when I invited her to go to Nebraska City with me to see *Hell's Angels*. That is, she couldn't have guessed at thirteen—or at thirty-five for that matter, when she had boys of her own to study and wonder about—what role she had been assigned to play in my intense imaginative life. She might have expected that I would try to kiss her in the car while we were riding home from Nebraska City with my brother and his date after the movie was over. Certainly I meant to do that and probably try to put one of my hands where she would eventually have breasts like Jean Harlow's. At thirteen she was prepared to sink her nails in my impudent hand and laugh it off with a merry, "None of *that!*"

But it was not a physical assault on her that I planned or needed. I was going to ravish her mind. With the aid of this powerful movie plus a few tickles and kisses afterward, I was going to wheedle her mind right away into the realm of wish and nonsense, where I was so lonely all by myself.

I had been making myself at home there since I had first begun to understand what this movie was going to be about. Of course I hadn't seen it yet, but months before I had read about it—probably in *Silver Screen*—and seen pictures of Jean Harlow in white furs with those big, bruise-toned spots under her eyes, of the burning Zeppelin, and of the Sam Browne-belted heroes who tangled with both.

There had been a bit of verse in the piece I read:

> *Hell's angels,*
> *Soaring in the central blue,*
> *As though to conquer Heaven*
> *And plant the banner of Lucifer*
> *On the most high....*

It was the verse which provided the cipher or incantation that really took me out. Out *there*. Through the hot days of that summer there would be a lot of occasions when I was lying there with my bare naked thigh against the chill lineoleum, beating away with the Harlow picture propped up in front of me, and just before I came, in that instant of focused self-awareness when I had stopped listening for the sound of my mother moving in the kitchen or my father or brother entering the house, I would say, "In the central blue" and *be there*. I would be one of them. And I thought, wouldn't it be a lot happier if Betty would become one too and be out there with me, since she was a girl?

What? Beg pardon? Once again...? How did I think this mating in the central blue was going to take place?

No use asking. I am no longer a mystic, so I no longer know. I repeat, merely, that in those months before my fourteenth birthday I anticipated that with the help of *Hell's Angels* I was going to ravish Betty Carnahan's mind. Too bad that I can't give a more satisfactory explanation. Anyway, it was in the hope of mental ravishment that I made the date with her two weeks before the movie came and with breathless stealth arranged that the two of us would go over to Nebraska City with my brother and his girl to see it.

Hudson Fowler behaved despicably when he heard that I was taking Betty. He acted as if it was his right to go with me if I had found a ride. "Get your mind above your belt," he said. "What do you want to do intercourse with that little nitwit for?"

"I don't," I said. I was shocked on many counts. Shocked by so much resentment from him just because I wasn't asking him along. His odd choice of expression shocked me into awareness that there was a fishy unreality in my plans for Betty.

He saw he had me on the defensive. "You pretend you're just interested in the airplanes," he crowed.

"They're burning a two-million-dollar zeppelin in this one."

"While all the time you just want an excuse to see Jean Harlow's legs. Listen, I've got a notion to show Aunt Ellen that dirty magazine you gave me and see if she lets Betty go with you at all."

The dirty magazine he alluded to was my copy of the movie magazine with choice shots of Miss Harlow in her starring role. It could hardly have shocked Mrs. Carnahan into an interference with my date. Hudson, with unscrupulous insight into the uses I had put it to, was merely using it to discomfort me.

"All right. Go ahead and take her," he said savagely. "But just remember this. Whatever happens over there"—he made *over there* sound splendidly more like Flanders Fields than like Nebraska City—"I've already done intercourse with her."

In the face of such challenge I had to claim, "Well, so have I."

"At the family reunion in Sidney. Behind the rodeo barns."

"At the Halloween party. On the school fire escape," I said.

Then we both called each other liars and backed away, throwing sticks and bits of bark and finally good sized rocks at each other's heads.

I should have known he wouldn't let it go at that. He got to my brother and with some sort of specious implication that I, his best friend, wouldn't dream of seeing this great movie without him, he arranged to go with us. Having conned my brother, Hudson insinuated to Betty and his Aunt Ellen that I hadn't so much been asking for a date as offering to share a historical cultural experience with Betty when I invited her to the movie. I suppose that such an implication was welcome to Mrs. Carnahan, in spite of my good reputation.

At any rate, when I bounded up on the Carnahan's porch just before dusk on that cold December afternoon—freshly bathed and shivering and wearing just a dash of my mother's perfume—who should come out in answer to my knock but Betty *and* Hudson. I didn't know then what arrangements had been made behind my back. All I knew was that I couldn't stand there, practically within earshot of Mrs. Carnahan and Betty's father, and go through the argument about Betty with Hudson again. He had me.

He had me good, and the rest of the evening was just one failing attempt after another to retrieve what I could from the disastrous misunderstandings he had set going. At least on the ride over Betty sat between Hudson and me in the back seat of the Essex. I fancied that she got a whiff or two of me in spite of the strong perfume she was wearing. Hudson and I bellowed the Air Force song back and forth for her benefit. In the front seat Betheen Hesseldahl, the big, cowy girl my brother was going with then, alternately nuzzled her face in his neck and sat as far away from him as she could move, asking for a cigarette. "Not in front of the kids," he growled. "Later," he promised. I managed to get my arm up on the back of the seat behind Betty for a mile or two. The trip over wasn't so bad.

But when we went into the theater things got horribly disarranged. I hung back politely to let the others slide into their seats first, and then found that Hudson was sitting between Betty and me. I could feel my bowels begin to writhe and burn. I leaned to Hudson's ear and called him a sonofabitch.

He caught me hard in the ribs with his elbow. "Ssssh! Look! There she is. Just like in the magazine."

What was going on—as I understood later, perhaps years later, when my equilibrium was at least restored—was the famous scene in which Harlow gets into something more comfortable. That was going on for the others. I was down between the rows of seats trying to get a lock on Hudson's arm and force him out of his place. He was trying to pay no attention to me. He burst into loud cackles, whether at the sight of Jean Harlow in *negligee* or at my plight I have no idea.

The usher came to quiet us. For the rest of the movie I huddled

31

motionless. I wouldn't have trusted myself to try to speak, even at the break after the feature. My brother sidled out past me to get popcorn for everyone and muttered, "What's the matter with you?" but I didn't answer him. Hudson said, "Boy, it really got me when that little plane came in over that big dirigible. You know it was *real.*" The sneak knew he had gone too far with me and was trying to make up, but I didn't even turn my head.

It was my impression that I didn't see a single bit of the movie. Only, afterward, as we were driving out of Nebraska City across that high, silvery bridge with the dry moon coming up over the Iowa bluffs, I began to get images that must have been before my eyes in the theater. Between the struts of the bridge I saw the RAF insignias and the snapping ribbons from the ailerons as the flight leader brought his planes up alongside us. There were black, darting shapes down where the silhouette of willows cut the reflecting glitter of ice near the Iowa shore.

A little later—not in any sequence that would have appeared in the film—I saw the Krauts in their zeppelin panic and prepare to cut loose the observation car dangling a mile below them over London. I was in that little teardrop contraption and I knew what they were doing. There was no way to stop them. Only a fool would have let himself in for such a mission.

And then Harlow was all over me. Her silks were jiggling like moonlight on my retinas and that white hair was moving in like a cloud on a high wind. The bruise-toned shadow of her cleavage was so close to my face that my eyes crossed trying to keep it in focus. I turned to Betty. She was leaning back quite peaceably in the crook of Hudson's shoulder. Her eyes were open and as far as I could make out, she was smiling. Hudson's free hand was stuck in between the buttons of her winter coat.

What I did then was inexcusable. That is, it is the kind of thing for which one's own psyche never, never finds a tolerable excuse, so that when you say to yourself long afterward, "Why I was only a fumbling, ignorant kid then," still the eye of memory averts itself.

While she leaned back in Hudson's arms, I tried to neck her. I tried to kiss her while his face was so close to hers that I could feel his hot breath on my cheek. I tried to unbutton her coat, not so much to get his hand out of it as to get mine in too.

"What are you little monkeys *doin'* back there?" Betheen Hessendahl wanted to know. She leaned over the back of the seat and giggled.

"You're crazy," Betty said.

"He's gone crazy," Hudson said, with maddening self-assurance. "Too much Harlow."

"Well, give everyone a cigarette," Betheen suggested.

My brother argued that the smell of tobacco would stay in the car and displease our parents. But in a minute he pulled to the side of the road and lit two. He gave one to Betheen and kept the other himself. After two drags she leaned back and passed it to us.

She passed it to Betty Carnahan, rather, and I can not describe the horror and excitement I felt when Betty leaned forward and puckered her lips to draw on it. It was not I who had had too much Harlow. It was Betty. Her mind had, somehow, been truly ravished by what she had seen. In the red glow from the cigarette a positively obscene merriment flickered over her little face. It was quite beyond anything I had meant for her. At that moment, and only then, I believed that she had been behind the rodeo barns at Sidney with her cousin.

I made up my mind then and there that after we had dropped Hudson at his house I would ask my brother to take Betty and me straight home. I knew it was his habit to take Betheen or one of his other girls to park down behind the grain elevator in an empty field at the end of his Sunday night dates, and in all the arrangements for this evening I thought it had been tacitly assumed that Betty and I might go there with them tonight. Now I didn't want to go. My mixed intentions had begun a process of depravity that had to be stopped. I wanted to go back to the innocence of that evening earlier in the fall when I had kissed Betty by the fire escape and run away.

Caught in such unfathomable hypocrisy, I hardly noticed that my brother stopped the car first in front of our house at the edge of Chesterfield.

"Good night," Betty said. "Thanks for the movie."

My brother said, "Hurry up. If the folks are awake they might look out and see we're back."

I said, "No."

They coaxed, they argued, they scoffed. That is, Betheen and my brother did—for guessable motives wanting me out of the car so they could quickly leave the other two at Betty's door. And when persuasion got them nowhere, they made the mistake of trying to extract me from the rear seat by force.

I was too stubborn to see that nothing remained to be salvaged from the evening. I simply clung and kicked. I grabbed indiscriminately at the upholstery, the window cranks, and Betty. Once I caught bïg-shouldered Betheen under the chin with my knee. In her recoil she cracked her head on the door frame. A pretty brawl!

They were still tugging uselessly when my father came out. He was wearing his old bathrobe with galoshes over his bare shins. I guess he'd thought we were having some trouble with the car when he started out into the cold.

"Why, you ought to be ashamed," he said to me as he grasped the real nature of our trouble. "Why, Betty's cousin can see that she gets home safe."

"I'd have let him come along if he hadn't put up such a fuss," my brother said. "He kicked Betheen."

"Gee, my mother will worry if I don't get home soon, 'cause tomorrow's a school day," Hudson said.

"Good night," Betty said, with just a precocious hint of sophistication.

Ah, I was ashamed all right. Ashamed of the whole sick, sorry human race as I walked through the frosty yard with my father. The tail lights of the Essex were already disappearing around the corner of the Christian church.

My father threw his arm around my shoulder. He wasn't as foolish or as hypocritical as his remark had made him sound. It was just that he, too, saw no way out of the tangle except to subtract me from it. It had gone beyond considerations of justice. All that remained was to restore order. "You'll see Hudson and Betty at school tomorrow," he said. "You'll see them every day. Things'll go better if you just forget what happened tonight."

I didn't answer.

"Now then, you're too old to cry," he said.

"Well, I'm crying, you bastard."

I expected him to hit me then. In fact you might say I had invited it and would have welcomed the punishment for having been such an idiot.

But he couldn't bring himself to do it. We were standing on the porch by then, and I saw him in fuzzy silhouette against the moonlit yard. I saw him waver as though he were lifting his fist but couldn't quite make it, and then, maybe for the first time, I saw him in his human dimension, bewildered and tugged in contrary directions like me.

"We better get some rest." That was the only moral he could draw from what he had just seen.

You remember that at the end of *Hell's Angels* there is a sequence in a German prison. One of the fly-boy brothers—of course it is the one who *missed* the hanky-panky with Miss Harlow in London that night the zep came over and she got into her comfort suit—has to shoot his sibling with a pilfered Luger to keep him from betraying plans for the spring offensive to the enemy. There's a lot of poetic justice in the shooting. One is made to feel the traitor should have kept it in his pants whatever provocations the Sexual Adversary offered. Morality is vindicated with bookkeeping precision. With the Luger still smoking in his hot little hand, the killer sniffles about *mein bruder* to a baffled Hun.

It has taken me a terrific, lifelong integrative effort to resurrect a memory of that movie with even a tint of morality or poetic justice. The images that first stuck with me composed a very different pattern. That night I lay under the covers sleeplessly waiting for my brother to come home, agonizing the minutes it would take him to get rid of Betty and Hudson, the minutes it would take to wheel down past the elevator for a quick feel and a kiss, and the other minutes to deliver Betheen home and come back.

I had no weapon to commit a physical murder with. But as plainly as if it were on a silver screen I could see myself hauling a Luger out of the bedclothes as he entered the room and began to undress. I would sneer, *"Mein bruder,"* and let him have it between the eyes. After him, the others, one by one. Then—"spinning through stardust and sunshine"—down I'd go. Down, down, down. Where, after all, my true desires had been tending.

The Father

This began many years ago. Since its origin was from an accident and since many of the consequences would never be duplicated, it may stand as a unique little history without much relation to the fated march of public events or the destinies of most people.

It began on a March morning when Cory Johnson was shelling corn in the crib of his farm. He had a rattletrap old sheller that he was rather proud of. Some of its parts—the gears and the rust-pitted fly-wheel bored for a hand crank—had come from a machine in use on this farm for longer than Cory had lived. But he had rebuilt the frame and replaced the shelling spikes inside. He had rigged an elec-tric motor and a system of belts to run the apparatus after the REA brought the wires out on this mail route west of Boda.

The sheller worked well enough. When there was no load of corn hitting the spikes, the rising and falling hum of the motor and the sibilance of the belts on the pulley faces were reasonably quiet. Of course, when corn was actually being shelled, a deafening racket filled this solid-walled room in the corner of the slatted crib.

Cory thought he was alone on the farm at this hour. His wife had taken all three children with her in the Model A. The two older boys were in school and would not come home until later afternoon. His wife hoped to drive into Boda to see her parents if the roads had not thawed too badly. She meant to take Bobbie, the youngest boy, along with her. Probably those two would not be back much before noon.

Cory liked being alone on his place. The job he had laid out for himself this morning was not pressing. At midmorning he would go to the house for coffee and cold pancakes with jelly. While he ate the snack he meant to listen to a science program broadcast daily from the station of the state university. He liked science. In his rural isolation he believed—then, early in the thirties, almost a full century after it began to dominate the life of the western world—that science was "the coming thing."

As he fell into the rhythm of it, he was enjoying his work as much as he ever had. The warming day, which would probably take the bottom out of the gravel roads between here and town before it was through, permitted him to take off his sheepskin coat. He was warm enough in a sweater as long as he kept busy, and for a good hour he worked without pause, bringing tin bushels full of corn from a pile in the slatted corncrib and feeding it into the machine.

While the ears ran down the trough to the hopper, Cory sometimes watched the throat of the outlet where the shelled grains poured into gunnysacks. Mostly the grains flowed out in a brisk, placid stream, but now and then above the main flow some single grains would leap like fast, yellow sparks from a grinding wheel. There was of course nothing extraordinary in the maverick behavior of these grains. They were the ones that had caught somehow between the cobs and the whirling spikes just long enough for elastic and centrifugal forces to build up, then hurl them like bullets ricocheting out the metal chute that filled the sacks. Still, their unpredictable flight suggested mysteries beyond the fringe of his experience. He had read in *Popular Science Monthly* where some Jap had invented a centrifugal machine gun. It pleased him mildly to think he was watching the principle of the gun being demonstrated by the apparatus he had put together. In another issue of the same magazine he had seen a photograph of electrons leaping through the dark of an experimental chamber, and though these pictures had showed no more than the scratch of a white line across a black rectangle, it pleased him to believe that electrons *really* looked like these hard-flung, zinging grains of corn.

Once that morning when Cory went out into the main storage bins of the crib to fill his bushels, he heard the electric motor change pitch. Its normal whine became a level, unpleasant hum. The slap and hiss of the driving belts had stopped. The motor was no longer turning over, and he had better shut down the current quickly before the armature burned out.

As he skipped for the door, the motor began to run again. A belt whistled on an immobilized pulley.

He saw his four-year-old son Bobbie standing beside the fly wheel with his gloved hand raised to the gear reduction. The boy's face was turned back over his sheepskin collar, and he was grinning the not quite honest grin he often showed when caught doing something destructive and forbidden—he grinned as if trying to minimize his offense.

Cory thought the boy had pushed a cob into the gears, experimentally, and thus had stopped the whole complex of machinery cold.

Then with a hawking scream that scalded his throat and the inside of his nose with bile, Cory called his wife's name. The boy's hand was in the gears. Down the fringed and starred cuff of his glove, blood was oozing briskly onto his sleeve and down the sleeve to the hem of his coat.

Cory had turned the power off and knelt with the boy in his arms by the time his wife ran from the car she had just parked.

As pain returned to the shocked nerves of the hand, the boy's grin merely enlarged until his mouth stood in a ridged O like the corolla of a white flower. He was now shrieking incessantly in fear and pain. He danced in his father's arms and jerked and jerked to free his hand. Urine bubbled through his overalls and mixed with the blood under his boots.

"Daddy'll get you out," Belle Johnson shouted in the boy's face.

"Daddy, Daddy, Daddy, Daddy," she moaned to Cory, depending like the child on his act to save them.

"Hold'm," Cory said. He vaulted the machine and knocked the belt from the drive shaft, vaulted back and set his shoulder to a spoke of the flywheel. When the gears moved, the boy shrieked louder and fainted.

"I'll take the sonofabitch apart," Cory said. He looked under the motor table for his toolbox. He remembered having put it in the trunk of the car. He was not sure whether he had left it there or had taken it out later in the barn.

"Daddy, he's swallowing his tongue," Belle said.

Cory put a finger and thumb in the boy's mouth. It was like

putting them into an electric socket with the current on. The strength of the curling tongue seemed greater than any he could force into his own hand.

It took him five seconds to secure the tongue and press his wife's nails into it. He believed it had taken two or three minutes.

Sweat was blinding him. He thought the boy might die if he did not hurry, but he caught himself staring with revulsion at the machine, taking time to blame himself not only for the failure to enclose the gears in a safety box, but for making anything so ugly and rough— for presuming to do something that only factory technicians working for pay could do right.

He fished out his jackknife and cut away the blood-sopped glove from the jammed hand. He thought it possible that the jersey might have cushioned the bones at least. What he saw looked like boiled and shredded chicken in which a bad cook had left bits of gristle and bone.

"Daddy, his mouth is turning blue," Belle said.

"All right. Hold onto him. Hold him tight," Cory said.

He took a dark-bladed hatchet from its hanging place on the wall. There was not much room for it between the gears and the bottom of the hopper. With a three-inch blow he clipped the hand just above the wristbone.

"Get a tourniquet on him. I'll get the car," he told his wife.

The doctor in Boda, young Doctor Grant, said that Cory had done a pretty good job of amputation, all things considered.

"Bobbie probably never even felt what you did," Doctor Grant said, with his clean, pink-nailed fingers resting on Cory's sleeve. "There was quite a little shock. Naturally. But if his hand was so badly mangled you couldn't get it free, you can be sure that's where the shock came from. Say, it didn't take you long to get him in here to me," he said with an encouraging gleam of admiration in his eyes.

"No," Cory said. "I just didn't pay any attention to the mudholes. I came through the bad stretch the other side of the bridge doing about sixty-five, I guess."

The doctor laughed quite loudly. "I'll bet you jumped that Model A right over the bad spots."

Now that he knew his boy was going to be all right—which at the moment meant that he was going to live—Cory felt an unaccountable but decent pride in his behavior after the accident. By God, he had held back nothing. He had ripped the guts out of his Model A, coming in from the farm in just seventeen minutes. By God, he had seen the mail carrier—the mail carrier, mind you—out beside his car studying the mire of gravel and standing water in the low spot beyond the creek and probably deciding it had thawed too bad for him to get the mail through. Now Cory could remind himself—what he wouldn't bend the doctor's ear with—that Belle had shouted from the back seat to go around the longer way by Hopewell Church when he took it on his own shoulders to give this way a try. He hated to think what might have happened if he had stuck the car in deep there, a mile and a quarter from town. And for a minute or two it had been touch-and-go with the mud geysering over his windshield and the car skidding always to the left against his pull on the steering wheel. He had seen the face of the mail carrier through a muddy window, puckered in disbelief, almost in awe, as he watched the Model A churn past him.

The car was still fishtailing uncontrollably when Cory took her up the bridge approach. The whipping rear end grazed half the girders of the span before he got her straightened. The rear bumper was gone and somewhere along the line he'd overtaxed the transmission so he couldn't get her shifted down from high when he had to wait for a truck to cross at the Boda stop sign. He killed the motor then and ran three blocks to the doctor's office with the boy in his arms and Belle unable to keep up with him. And made it in time.

In time. In time. In time. The thought quieted the thudding of his heart.

"I don't think there's enough loss of blood to worry us," Doctor Grant said. "The tourniquet worked very nicely." Doctor Grant was only concerned—just a little—about the effects of shock, he said. He wanted to drive the boy over to the hospital in the county seat as soon as he had seen two more patients. He wanted to make sure Bobbie had his strength built up "before I finish the job for you," as he put it to Cory, with a wink of complicity. The Johnsons could ride along in the doctor's car. Belle could hold the little fellow in her lap, and everything would be arranged so one of them could stay all night with him in the hospital.

In the meantime, while his parents waited, the boy was sleeping in one of the doctor's examination rooms. He had been given morphine. Everything seemed to be under control. The orderly flow of circumstance had resumed again.

Cory opened a magazine, there in the doctor's waiting room—not so much because he thought he could read anything just now as because he wanted some shield behind which to hide until he came to terms with himself. Most importantly, he had to choke down the boisterous, excessive pride that had come on the rebound of his relief. He kept wanting to grin when he thought of the mail carrier's face. But if he couldn't help grinning, no one ought to see him do it. Then, too, he might want to pray out some of his thanksgiving that the roads hadn't been too bad, that Doctor Grant knew his business, and so on. Cory was still religious in crisis, though in normal times he lived by the opinion that "a lot of people went too far" with the religious business.

"Cory?"

He heard Belle's whisper like something whispering to him out of the past—like his mother come to wake him for a fine day in summer after vacation from school had begun and he could enjoy himself helping *his* daddy around the farm.

He looked up from the magazine. Belle's face was so pale he was frightened for her. Her blue eyes looked black against her ghostly skin.

"Daddy," she said, "don't feel too bad. You had to do it."

Of course it would have occurred to him sooner or later, without any prompting from Belle, that he and he alone was guilty for the loss of Bobbie's hand.

Since Cory would rather—if wishes had anything to do with the matter—have given his own hand, the way the guilt came to present itself was especially hard for him to master.

The point wasn't his negligence. As his father-in-law said, "There's a great many dangerous things around a farm, Cory. There always will be for kids."

"I know it," Cory said. "There's got to be machinery and animals and the pony that Joe and Gordon ride. You take the windmill tower for an example. I've caught Joe and Gordon up there I don't know how many times. They might any time fall and break their necks. Or the fan's going and they stick their heads up through the platform. Pfffttt!"

The older man extended the rhythm of agreement. "That's a fact, and you know Belle, when she was little, one time I nearly toppled a horse tank I was loading right onto her." He shuddered even now.

"Ah, but Dad, you held it," Belle recalled.

"I did," her father said. "And I paddled you for it when I saw you were safe. And I always remembered what a scare I had. But the point is that accidents just happen, Cory. After all, that's what the word *accident* means."

44

"Yeah, it does," Cory said.

The conversation was one of a great many that took place in the spring and summer after Bobbie lost his hand. They amounted to a kind of informal funeral, commemorating and at the same time draining away the immediate emotions of loss. It appeared, even to Cory, that it did him good to speak of the accident. He found no difficulty in saying man to man, man to wife, father to children—even to Bobbie—that an accident was something that just happened. Cory knew as well as any man that this was so.

Though he said many times that he could shoot himself for not having put a safety box around those gears on the sheller, this negligence was not the point that proved most crucial, either.

"You should have done that," his father-in-law said once when Cory lamented the absence of such a guard. "Well, we go on and try to make up for our past mistakes, and it does seem kind of sad to lock the door after the horse is gone, but that's what we do. I notice you took some rungs out of the ladder up the windmill."

"And Gordon climbed it the other night anyway," Belle said. "Shinnied right up the frame and had to yell for Cory to come and get him off."

They laughed and Cory laughed with them. Yes. Just to go on living he had to accept the likelihood of accidents, particularly where boys were involved, and he could do that.

But it wasn't the accidental part of Bobbie's misfortune that settled permanently into Cory's mind, freezing it to a pattern of distress. What he could never face—could never understand—was that he was guilty in taking that hatchet down from its hanging place on the wall and cutting off his son's hand.

"You had to do it," Belle said. She was willing to repeat this assurance whenever she thought it would help.

It never helped. Cory knew he'd had to do it. But necessity was no excuse at all for the guilt that rode him. The more he rehearsed his motives, the less important they seemed in comparison with the immortal act. If it was only bad luck that had put him in a situation where he had no choice, still, that luck was *his*. The guilt seemed to reside in that simple fact.

"It's like if I'd been someone else, not any part of this awful thing would have happened," he said to Belle.

Now that her emotions had resumed their normal level, she was almost as much amused as concerned at this odd way of putting it. She probably thought he was fishing for sympathy, and though she didn't mind sympathizing with him all he wanted, she didn't know how to offer the right response to his fancy. She said, "Sure. Sure. If you were someone else you wouldn't have this farm. You wouldn't have your nice kids. You wouldn't be stuck with me. Well, that's all a pipe dream, old man. You're stuck with all of us, and we'll get along. You know we will. Bobbie's a brave little guy. We might just thank God he was always left-handed."

"I know we'll get along," Cory said.

"You shouldn't punish yourself this way, because there's nothing to punish yourself for."

"I know that too."

"Then don't get depressed like this."

He had not spoken from depression, but from guilt. He knew well enough what depression was. He was depressed in those years of the thirties when the drought took most of his corn crop two years in succession; when he let himself be cheated in buying a secondhand car that turned out to have a cracked block; when he had trouble with his gallstones and had to cripple around all one winter; when his oldest boy, Joe, had trouble with his high-school studies and went off to join the Navy; when Belle's father, a man who'd been so good to Cory and his family and so dear to Bobbie, died of cancer; when the war came and Joe was out there at Pearl Harbor, where the Japs dropped on them with their newfangled weapons, and so many didn't have a chance on the anchored ships.

Year by year there were things to depress him. Big things and little things. And through the same years there'd been good times and times of satisfaction when he *wasn't* depressed. Take the summer he'd put the family in the car and driven them out to Yellowstone Park. That trip was a pure satisfaction. He couldn't remember a thing wrong with it.

Easily he remembered the good winters when he and Gordon were teaching Bobbie to hunt with them. They would load the dogs in the back seat of the car and drive over to the creek bottom to look for rabbits, quail, or pheasants. Cory had his pump gun. Gordon and Bobbie "shared" the single-shot .410 that had been bought for Joe when he turned twelve. Off they'd mush through the snow and broken cornstalks, trying to keep up with the badly trained dogs, joking and trading insults like three men—or three boys, it didn't matter which. Once, Cory'd knocked down three cock pheasants from a rising covey. Bobbie clapped his mitten to the side of his head and howled in admiration and disbelief. "Purty good, for an old man," he yelled over the snow. "Purty good."

"Even if you did get more than the limit," Gordon put in. "You going to tell the game warden I shot one of them?"

What he'd seen in the boys' eyes that afternoon was unmistakable and worth treasuring—just standing there in the snow with the dead birds around them, the boys being proud of their old man. It was like the male satisfaction he'd felt the day he took Bobbie in through the mud to the doctor's. In time. Only now the boys were here to share and mirror back the lonely pride of his manhood.

There had also been the good times—not to mention *all* the blessings of the years—when Joe came home on boot leave; when prices picked up in thirty-nine and the same year Belle had another boy, Cory Jr.; and when they got the first letter from Joe after Pearl Harbor saying he was all right.

The good things and the bad things of an ordinary farmer's life had happened to him. He had responded to them like an ordinary man, with satisfaction or depression.

But the guilt he endured was something else. It seemed to have a life of its own, to be almost a distinct life he lived when his ordinary life gave him the opportunity.

Weeks, months, years went by in which he forgot that he was guilty. During those periods he got quite used to Bobbie's disfigurement, as if it were a condition that had always existed, one intended by nature.

Fortunately, Bobbie wasn't the boy to feed on sympathy. He managed. As far as his parents could tell, he was a happier boy than Joe had been.

Cory watched without sentimentality as his maimed son grew up. But when the awareness of his guilt came back in one of its cyclic manifestations, he found that it had not diminished with time. After ten years it was as keen and lively as it had been that morning in Doctor Grant's office when Belle had unintentionally announced it to him.

An assortment of events served, through the years, to recall it, the way symptoms in the throat announce the approach of a general systemic infection.

For example, there was Bobbie's fight in the school yard when he was in the second grade.

Cory saw most of the mix-up. Driving homeward from an errand in Boda, he and Gordon stopped to pick up Bobbie from his play after school. From where the car was parked, they could see some boys darting back and forth beyond the schoolhouse, dodging, turning, skidding in the grass, swinging at each other in what seemed to be a game of tag. Then Glen Horstman chased Bobbie down into the corner by the well. Bobbie backed into the hedge separating the school yard from a cornfield. He sparred away the jabs and pokes the bigger boy aimed at him. It looked as if both boys were laughing breathlessly, having a lot of fun.

They saw Glen Horstman feint a kick and follow the feint with a blow of his fist that started Bobbie's nose bleeding. Bobbie signaled that he'd had enough: *Lay off. I surrender.*

Glen kept punching. He had knocked Bobbie to the ground and was sitting on him when Gordon leaped the ditch and went running to the rescue.

Laggardly, Cory followed. He was only a few steps from the car when he saw Gordon chase Glen into the schoolhouse.

"Gordon!" he commanded.

Gordon stopped on the wooden stairs by the door and turned. His face was quizzical and angry. "Why, I'll just knock *him* around a little bit," he said.

"No you won't," Cory told him. "You and Bobbie come on and get in the car now. Bobbie'd better wash his face at the pump."

"But he's bigger than Bobbie," Gordon said. He blushed because he did not want to mention that Bobbie lacked one hand to use in self-defense.

"Get in the car!" Cory shouted.

All the way home from the schoolhouse, Gordon sat in incredulous, wounded silence. Bobbie, though, was talkative enough. He wasn't in any pain from his beating. He wasn't really mad at Glen Horstman. Now that it was over, the fight seemed to him a pure entertainment.

But that, as Gordon's silence implied, was not all that must be taken into account. On almost any other day he would have been there at school to protect his brother. At least, without his father's inexplicable attitude to reckon with, he would have known what he ought to do tomorrow.

After supper, Gordon went to his mother about what had happened. She, in turn, spoke furiously to Cory as soon as the boys were in bed.

"I think I'd just better get on the telephone and find out from his teacher if this has ever happened before—the kids picking on Bobbie. I won't have it. Just because he's crippled—"

"Aw, Belle, that wasn't why Glen done it. They was playing and he got carried away."

"Playing? Gordon said he hit Bobbie with his fist. He was sitting on him, pounding his head, and you didn't...." She didn't say what Cory should have done that he had omitted, but she shook her head bitterly. The more she thought, the more worked up she got.

"Well, you go ahead and call the teacher if you want to put your nose in it," Cory growled.

"I *will* put my nose in it," she said, "and you'd better go over to the Horstmans' place and have a little talk with Glen's dad, because I don't intend to have this kind of thing going on, whatever you intend."

"But Bobbie wouldn't want—"

"You can drive me over and sit in the car while I go in and have it out with them," she raged. "You can sit in the car if you're scared to tell Ralph Horstman we want this stopped."

The Horstman farm was less than a two-mile drive. Through the spring night and the murmur of a rainy wind, Cory drove slowly, telling himself that of course Belle was right. He sighed heavily and thought he'd want his friends who lived around him to come and tell him about it if one of his boys had done a wrong. But he seldom felt so uneasy about anything as he did walking in under the elms of the Horstman yard and knocking at the screen door of the back porch.

"He what? Glen done *what?*" Ralph Hortsman bellowed. He grabbed Cory's shoulder and dragged him in from the back porch to the kitchen. "When'd he do that? This afternoon?" Horstman's throat began to swell rhythmically. He seemed to be growing taller and broader. "Mama, give Cory a cup of coffee or—or some *beer!*" he shouted to his wife. Then he fled the kitchen, pounding up the stairway from the living room like a plow horse frenzied in a burning building.

Cory and Mrs. Horstman heard the thump of a body dumped from its bed onto the floor and then a long, sleepy, uninterrupted wail, accompanied irregularly by the sound of slaps. In a minute Mrs. Horstman ran upstairs, too.

More slaps then. A more complicated sound of struggle began as the woman tried to mediate. Again and again, like the boom of outraged justice itself, Ralph Horstman's voice shouted, "He hit li'l Bobbie!"

After the condemnation, the smack of a hand on a rump, and then the woman's plea, seeming only to convince her husband that she had not understood the enormity of the offense. "But he hit li'l Bobbie!"

Downstairs Cory listened in what he could no longer doubt was envy. He knew well enough what he had no wish and no way of explaining to Gordon or Belle—that when he had seen Glen Horstman's fist bring blood from Bobbie's nose, he had felt a merciless identification with the aggressor. He had been unmanned by the recognition.

He had not wanted Bobbie hurt. No! He had never wanted Bobbie hurt, but he had seen his own act reenacted and known himself as powerless to prevent the pain as before.

But Glen Horstman, because he was a little boy, could be punished for what was, after all, a small offense. Cory, for his immeasurably greater offense, could expect no such squaring of accounts.

Afterward, each time his guilt flared in his face, he had to endure it in the same way until, mysteriously, it faded in his mind again—not dead, not even eroded by the remorse he had paid for it, merely waiting to be wakened again and endured again like an operation submitted to without anesthetic because, though he was guilty, no one owed him punishment.

He was punished. In the last year of the war, Gordon had just been drafted and sent to Fort Bragg when Joe was killed near Okinawa. By that time Joe was a seaman first class serving on a destroyer escort. The DE was on picket duty about seventy miles east of Buckner Bay when it was attacked by a George fighter. The attack occurred near sundown. A broad highway of gold and choppy crimson opened away from the little ship toward the west. The fighter came down this road like an erratic spark of gallantry and panic, hurled without conscious aim. The big ring sights on Joe's 20-mm. cannon must have circumscribed the sun itself as he swung it over to defend the ship. The fighter struck just abaft and below the bridge. The ship lived for several hours more, time enough for the survivors to be transferred to a destroyer. None of Joe's shipmates saw him or his body after the attack.

When the news came to the Johnson farm, Cory wept like any father bereft. And his tears were partly tears of relief, for it seemed to him in the first debility of sorrow that this extravagant punishment might, at last, pay off his guilt. It was not even in his heart to protest that the payment was too great, though he saw no equivalence between the hand he had taken from one child and the life he must now yield helplessly back to darkness. If he was quits, he must be satisfied.

But when the grief diminished and his strength returned, Cory saw that whatever had happened to Joe had nothing to do with his old guilt, which was neither increased not minimized by Joe's death. What little religion Cory had kept through the years melted with this discovery. Religion seemed foolish to him now, a windy pretense at linking things that had no real connection. The issue was between himself and a chaos to which only a fool would pray.

He had nothing with which to replace religion. His irregular and shallow enthusiasm for science had long since vanished of its own inanity. Besides, though science had once seemed to him "the coming thing," he had never been notified that science might pretend to explain what he thirsted terribly to know. It had been fun to read about the novelties science discovered. He had got bored. That was all.

In his whole life, as he could look back at it now, only one condition had given meaning to his work and the depressions or satisfactions that went with it. That condition was his fatherhood. Even if he had fathered his boys more or less accidentally, in lust, in lukewarm fondness for his wife, his fatherhood had come to be more than the sum of days and of forgotten wishes. Before anything else, he was a father—and it was against this definition of himself that he had been forced to strike that day in the corncrib.

Belle died in 1950. Cory wept for her, too; envied her, too, for he suspected she must have carried through life some secret, like his, of undiminishable guilt for rebellion against the self that time and accident had given her. But now she was free of it.

They said Cory's mind began to fail him after Belle's death.

His mind was working better than ever—and he understood that was what his family and Doctor Grant *meant*, though they had to express themselves by an exact inversion of the truth.

If they had said he was troublesome and a bit frightening to live with, he could have agreed straightforwardly. But they needed more than that. Like most people, they needed a shallow burrow of "reasons" and "explanations" because they dared not deal with a sheer, objective fact. He could no longer live on their sort of explanations, but he sympathized with them. So he said, Yes, he reckoned his mind was going back on him. He didn't want to be a trouble to them, and if he couldn't straighten up by himself, he would certainly do what Doctor Grant recommended. He would go to the asylum "for a while." In the meantime, while they gave him a chance, he wanted to carry on his share of the work on the farm.

In this period there were five of the family living together there. Cory, Bobbie and his wife Lucy, and their little boy Ed (after Lucy's father), and Cory, Jr. Between them, Bobbie and Cory, Jr. could just about take care of the farm work. Bobbie had been to Ag school at the state university and he was a fine manager, very good with book-work and planning ahead about the crops and machinery and soil, and figuring how they could afford the new things they needed. Farm work was more and more a matter of business brains these days, and he was sure that Bobbie was all right in that department.

Bobbie had got himself a new device to use for a right hand, too, now that they could afford it. There had been so much more money coming in during and after the war! Now you take Joe, Cory would tell himself, we just couldn't have afforded to send him to the university, Mother and I, back when he might have wanted to go. Then, quicker than anyone else could have reminded him that Joe was not a great one for study or using his brain, Cory would throw in that very qualification and go on: Yes, but things are getting so well-organized that they can take a boy who's not so bright to begin with and kind of guide him over the hurdles and give him remedial work and guide him into the right niche and he does all right! This was the way Cory's mind went on and on in an endless series of examinations and connections. His mind was far from failing. It dealt with more all the time, and, insofar as the mind alone was concerned, it was dealing more effectively. The sickness was elsewhere.

What Bobbie had was too grand and clever to be called a hook, though he good-humoredly called it that on weekdays. On Sunday, for fun, he called it a prosthesis. It was really three hooks and a bar, all with a bright chromium finish that twinkled wonderfully in the May morning sun when the young man swung himself up onto the tractor seat and headed out to the fields, while Lucy held little Ed and waved to him from the back door.

It was so strange, sometimes, to Cory to see that shiny batch of levered claws on the baby's back when Bobbie was holding him—as at the homecoming picnic in Boda when there was a crowd and the Johnsons drove in to see all their old friends come back to this hick town. Gordon was with them, too, on that occasion, visiting a week from his job in Seattle, where he'd remained with an opportunity after the service.

That *thing* on the baby's back would look just as firm and tender as a human hand. Odd how Bobbie could use it to caress with sometimes, as if it were alive, though of course it had no sense of touch. It could express feeling though it had none. The only time the baby minded being touched with it was in cold weather. But Cory's thoughts were often busy on conjectures as to whether the baby *ought* to mind being touched by the lifeless thing. No end to considerations involved there.

With his prosthesis Bobbie could manage nearly any chore on the farm. No doubt if worse came to worst, everything could be handled without hired help if Cory went away. But Cory had made his place, now that the boys were taking over so much, by doing the dirty and menial jobs that their machinery still left undone. True, they had a milker, and even Cory, Jr. could handle the milking of their twelve cows without complaining he had been put upon. Someone still had to shovel up after the stock. The boys rented a corn picker from the elevator in Boda for the corn shucking. Someone had to drive the tractor into town through a November rain to get the picker and see that it got back on schedule. Cory always did jobs like that.

Doctor Grant didn't like it much that Cory should make himself into a nigger—that was his word—for the boys. As he saw it, this was another symptom of Cory's mental deterioration. But the doctor's opinion on this account was only one way of looking at it, and Cory was very well aware of this.

He realized that quite aside from any help he gave with the work or any hardship he imposed on Lucy by giving her another mouth to cook for, he *worried* his family.

He was sorry for this, but deliberately he went ahead with his alarming and aberrant courses. In the winter of 1952 he spent part of every day in the corncrib, where he was reconstructing the corn sheller that used to stand in the corner room. He scoured the neighborhood and the junk piles around Boda for old parts. He rebuilt the wooden frame where the electric motor had sat. He drilled bolt holes in the concrete floor he and Gordon had poured back in wartime when they junked the old sheller. He begged some secondhand lumber from the people who had moved onto the Horstman farm, not wanting to spend any more good money than he had to on his "foolishness."

It took Bobbie less than a week to figure out what his father was doing—a little longer to decide to intervene. Then one morning he made a point of sauntering down to the crib and entering the room where his father was hammering and sweating.

"What you up to?" Bobbie said. "I thought since I didn't have much to do this morning, maybe I could...."

The brightness and pretense—from both sides—faded quickly enough. A reckless pity shone from Bobbie's face. He wet his lips.

"Dad, you're making that sheller again, isn't that it?"

"Well, Bobbie, yeah, I thought I'd run her up again and see if maybe I could improve the design. Like you say, there's not too awful much work to be done these days, though maybe I ought to be down at the barn having a look at that loader Cory broke last summer." He started to leave the room.

Bobbie stopped him. "I didn't mean that, Dad. You don't have to work every minute. But—but, it seems kind of useless for you to be making a sheller."

"Yeah, it does."

"Then—"

"It kind of—"

"Dad, Lucy and I've been talking and we want you to, well, go out to Seattle and see Gordon awhile. You keep saying it would cost too much, and Seattle's a big place if you don't want to stay with Gordon. Look, I'm going to come right out with it. Lucy and I don't feel right for having called Doctor Grant in on you. Doctors don't know everything. But a family is different, and I know that Gordon would want you to come."

"—kind of helps me think things out," Cory said mildly, touching the homely machine he was building. "I'm not a hand like you are to put things down on paper or in words, either, and if I can build something to see, that helps with my brain work."

Bobbie gritted his teeth. "But you're thinking about things you ought to leave alone," he said. He held up his claw, glittering and lightly sweating in the cold room. "You're brooding about *this* again. For my sake, leave it alone. You think all my life I've blamed you somehow and I haven't. Can't you believe me when I say it? You *saved* my life and everyone knows that."

"I don't know," Cory said. "Maybe there was some other way to do it."

"*Was!*" The horror of that exploded syllable stood with them like the angel of death. What had been in time was not, any longer, in time. The past was unalterable, and yet they could not shake from their minds the illusion of free choice.

"I've had a good life," Bobbie said—as if that bore on the enigma that Cory wrestled. He might have had *another* life if his father had been the man to find another means of saving him. "What more could I want? I've been happy," Bobbie said.

"I know, son," Cory answered. "What I'll do, I'll get the pickup this afternoon and carry this junk down in the east forty and dump it. Guess I'd better save the lumber and use it for kindling."

Bobbie snarled in his frustration. "You don't have to do *that*, Dad. You don't have to do anything I tell you or anything for my sake. That's the point. Don't you get it?"

"Sure I see what you mean," Cory said. "I wasn't thinking about how you—and Lucy, I suppose—would feel about this contraption. Now let's just walk up to the house for some coffee and I'll tell Lucy

I'm sorry I started it."

Bobbie said, "Maybe you'd better not mention it to her."

"All right," Cory said. "Whatever you think is best."

The next morning he was working on the sheller again. He had got to the point of installing the gears and covering them with a steel safety box.

Probably his queer behavior and his family's concern with it had been going on longer than he realized. Because they cared for him they would have taken what pains they could not to let him notice their precautions. Noting their few failures to be discreet was like seeing an advance guard of rats begin to invade the farm. Experience had convinced him that if you saw only the signs of depredation, that meant there were ten rats around your buildings. If you saw one rat, that meant a hundred. If you saw two together, a thousand, probably.

Now, to all his other considerations, he added the task of measuring the impressions he made each day on Lucy, Bobbie, and Cory, Jr. Like a stock-market gambler he read the daily quotations of his stock with them. Better this afternoon. Low and worried this week. Cautious. Desperate. Better. Better. The same.

They could not bring themselves to wound him by flat and final decisions in his behalf. If Bobbie had really insisted, Cory would have packed and gone to Seattle. Probably he would never have come back from that city.

At the same time, he realized that he confused their impressions by the very act of measuring them. And if their sanity wavered to the magnetism of his craziness—as he saw it did—then how could he trust them for reliable guidance, even in what he ought to do?

He understood, sometime during 1953, that they had been cautioned by Doctor Grant—or another authority they might have consulted at Grant's recommendation—to be on the lookout for a suicide attempt. He knew this first by subtle signs, as he would have known about a family of rats in the corncrib before he saw the first darting black shape and prepared for a campaign of poison and traps. The subtle signs were followed by a blunder so loving and crude it made him weep.

One morning he found that his straight razor had disappeared from the cabinet in the bathroom and had been replaced with an electric shaver. The exchange had been made just one week before Christmas, and he knew the electric gadget had been bought as a present for him. In their anxiety they had been unable to wait.

He picked up the shaver without hesitation. He accepted whatever Lucy and Bobbie (or was it Lucy alone, weaker in her fear, who had

55

made the switch?) thought had to be done. He put the plug into an outlet and set the humming head to his cheek. He saw his cowed eyes under the windburnt sag of lids. It seemed to him his courage was not adequate to his pity.

"Father," he said, as he used to pray in the time he had not taken religion seriously enough to reject it. "Father." He heard no distinct syllables, but a shapeless groan.

The futility of their gesture seemed unendurable. They had taken his razor—didn't these children know that, on a farm, as Belle's Dad had put it, the means to harm were never lacking? He supposed they had hidden away the shells for his pump gun, too, though he had not bothered to check for some time. Odds and ends of rope had probably been gathered from the barn and outbuildings (by Bobbie, careful not to let on to Cory, Jr. why he was being so neat these days). They probably timed his comings and goings, not to permit him to be too long alone. And what good would all that do if he could claim the right to kill himself?

To put their minds at ease he wanted to go to them now and tell them how he had once determined to do away with himself and why that was all past. The occasion had come soon after Joe's death. The absence of the coffin from the funeral services had served as a reminder of the absence of justice due from the empty heavens. That had been more than eight years ago. No one had worried then about gathering up ropes from the sheds, garage, or barn.

He had put a rope around his neck one morning before anyone else was out of bed, standing by the square opening in the floor of the haymow. There was enough light at that hour to show the churchlike vaulting of rafters in the empty mow. Nothing had ever tempted him more seductively than the black square in front of his toes.

But he had taken the rope off with the slow deliberation of a judge —not for a moment assuming that he was granting himself reprieve, but that in all solemnity he was refusing it. Self-execution was inappropriate to his guilt.

Well—of course he must not go to the children and tell them what he remembered of that morning. He was poor with words; he was more likely to scare them than to appease them. They weren't prepared to understand that what he had sentenced himself to that morning in the barn was *to think*. Under that sentence, he was obliged to respect all the problems raised whenever he was rash enough to solve one of them.

He had to think, though it was not easy for him. It was not easy to rid the farm of a pestilence of rats, either, but, again and again through his years on this place, he had set himself the task of poisoning and trapping creatures who had over him the advantages of number, secrecy, and natures that recognized no obligation except to exist. He supposed there had never been a day when the farm was free of rats. Yet, by unwavering persistence he had thinned the rat population again and again to the point at which it was tolerable.

It wasn't easy for him to get ahead of the problem he now presented to his anxious children, but he set himself to find how to make it easier for them.

Through that spring and much of the following summer he appeared to be succeeding. The cycles of compulsive thought that had made him careless of his behavior since Belle's death sped faster—of necessity—as they seemed to settle down into the tranqulity of age. Once upon a time he would have refused to believe himself capable of the nimble calculations that now became a commonplace.

He gave up working on the sheller in the corncrib—because he had now got the whole material apparatus in his mind, from the grain of old wood to the bolts that fastened the electric motor to its bench, the pulleys and flywheel and their weight, strength, appearance, sound, and speed—all of this so completely transposed into an image that he could set the machine going in his imagination whenever he wanted. While he helped his youngest son with homework, or went over the accounts with Bobbie, or listened attentively to Lucy's frets about her new pregnancy, another part of his mind could repeat the crucial morning of his life.

So his family thought him better. They said he was "more himself" than he had been for years. They noticed how he gave up a share of the meanest work to each of his boys. Sometimes now he talked voluntarily of going to visit Gordon.

They were glad, again, to invert the truth. He saw that this second inversion did not cancel out the first—when they had believed him mad—but only made it incalculably more difficult to encompass, as if an already insoluble labyrinth should suddenly open out into its duplicate.

World without end, the world of thought that seemed bent on returning to some safe, lost starting point; but the prospect of its difficulty neither cheered nor daunted him. While he had strength of mind, he would go on as best he could, pretending that he was a juggler, an explorer, an acrobat, though he was only a big-footed farmer. At least he had learned to pace himself in his pursuit of multiplying complications. He had learned not to try too much at once. He was glad to think this adjusted pace—whether it meant success or failure to him—comforted his family.

One night in late summer he reached the end of thought. He had not foreseen (as a man with greater original gifts might have) that there could be an end of it. But there it was, confronting him. What had been a constantly accelerating series of wheels within wheels, wheels begetting wheels, a spinning and a spiraling that multiplied and exploded toward the ultimate horizons—all that was frozen in an instant into what seemed to him an immense sphere of light, motionless, achieved.

On the night it happened he was alone on the farm except for his grandson, who was sleeping upstairs. At suppertime Lucy had said with unusual petulance that she probably wouldn't get to go anywhere again for months or see any of their friends. The new baby was due soon. She would be tied down permanently after its arrival, so why didn't Bobbie take her anyplace any more?

Since he had been working hard in the hayfield all day, Bobbie might have snapped back at her. But Cory smoothed things over. He suggested that they drive through Boda to the county seat and find a place to dance or go to a movie. He was kind of tired himself, but would be glad to bathe Ed and read him a story and let him watch TV awhile before he went to bed.

Then Cory, Jr. had popped up and said he wanted to go along, too, and again there had been the threat of friction that Cory had to deflate judiciously. Why didn't young Cory ride just as far as Boda, he suggested, and drop off there to see some of his buddies? He could stay all night with Mickey Carnahan if he wanted, as a reward for working so well all day.

Cory had eased them away smoothly. The three young people left the farm after supper in a jolly mood. Young Ed had turned out to be no trouble at all. He nodded in front of the TV and went to bed early.

It was still not altogether dark when Cory took his cigar onto the screen porch to sit on the glider and do some thinking. On quiet evenings, left alone, he felt able to catch up on the arrears in his thought.

The night was faintly oppressive, though mild. He could hear the tree frogs dinning in the yard and the chug of the pump down by the barn. He heard the intermittent traffic of his neighbors going in late to Boda or the county seat, most of them traveling the new blacktop.

He thought about the highway and his neighbors and the way things had changed and the way things had been before. He thought, without emotion, of the difference between the blacktop and the muddy gravel he had charged through the day he cut off Bobbie's hand. Then he thought of the real sheller that had caused the accident and of the imaginary sheller that had duplicated it in his mind. And presently he was sure as could be that the sheller he imagined was run by the same principles that had run the sheller made of wood and steel. His creation and he were indistinguishable.

With that realization he reached the end of thought, knowing neither good nor evil but only guilt. The tree frogs, perhaps, continued their monotonous, hysterical song in the dark leaves around him. There may have been a continuing traffic on the roads and the sound of the pump's piston beating back and forth in its imprisoning cylinder. He did not hear them. Whatever existed was silent and motionless. Eternal. As it had been and as it would be when time ended.

In that silence he rose from the soft glider and let himself out the screen door onto the grass of the yard. He walked, without needing a light, to the shed by the back gate. The motion of his body was fluent and easy, but he felt nothing. It seemed to him that he was constituted of the same material as Bobbie's well-wrought hook and had been able, like it, to express love without the ability of knowing it. (The proposition was the same if exactly reversed: to know love without the ability to express it.) The only passion remaining was for a justice that would bring a man in phase with the total equilibrium of the night.

From the shed he took a short ax and went upstairs to his grandson's bedroom. He came down a little later without it.

He sat in the glider and relit his cigar. After a while he found himself straining to hear the tree frogs. To hear anything. Because he was not dead he had to break the motionless, soundless sphere of the thoughtless universe. He needed a noise to start him thinking again.

It was peaceful enough not to think—just to suck on the sweet cigar and let it all go up in a gentle exhalation. But he had to resume, if he could, the pain of thought so he could review what he had done in that silence when the sound of machinery stopped.

He had to plan the right way to present his act, or all those folks who relied on explanations would refuse to believe him sane. If they did not believe him sane, they would not punish him for this repetition of his guilt, and if he could not trick those who ought to love him into responsibility for a just punishment, then there was no hope for him in all this vast gleam of silence.

Hatcher's Devil

The more charitable folks in town agree that John Elwood deserted his family because he was driven past endurance by the behavior of his fifth child, a boy named Hatcher.

John's deserted wife, Virginia, supports this view. She was neither embittered nor, as it turned out, inconvenienced by this abandonment, so she found no need to recall the affront it had given her. In all these years afterward, though she has had no evidence that he has not died, she has spoken of John as of one who was swiftly transposed to another sphere of existence by powers beyond mortal control. She never said that John had "passed away." Only some undertone of her remarks suggested that she believed he had.

Sometimes, to whatever sympathetic lady of the town or curious relative who dug for an explanation, Virginia would summarize her trouble like this: "John was never a worried man but for that one funny year. And then—I just believe he lost all his *faith* in things.

Lost it altogether.'' Then she would smile her fragile charity across the teacups and drop her hands submissively into her lap. "He'd been in such a stew about our Hatcher I think he let it get him.'' And since the friends or relatives were generally informed about Hatcher by common gossip they inquired no further.

Until he was seven Hatcher had given no one any memorable trouble. Perhaps he had not yet understood as precisely as he wished what crime is, for he was a weak child and learned everything with difficulty. He seldom asked questions. When he did they were apt to be oblique or absurd and never in that awkwardly coherent kind of series that most children manage. "What's that *for*?'' he might ask, pointing at the ground under his feet, at a page of a newspaper, or looking at a car passing in the street. If no answer was possible, he'd grin wisely, drop his translucent eyelids, and nod as though he'd learned something from the lack of an explanation.

"Who are the Elwoods?'' he would demand of his brothers and sisters. They thought this was funny or that he had an odd substitute for a sense of humor, or that he was mentally bad off. This latter was not quite a fair estimate, though it was truly said that he was slower than most children in learning right from wrong.

Once he had learned, he chose wrong like a duty. He went at it furiously on a scale that our little town was not prepared for. His first job was on the neighbors who lived across the garden from the Elwoods. They were a kindly old couple who made pets of all the Elwood children, their own being grown and gone.

Hatcher walked into their kitchen one spring evening when they were spading a flower bed in the front yard and took eighteen dollars in bills from a sugar bowl.

The money was missed the same evening, and the neighbors came lamenting their trouble to the Elwoods. They didn't think of course that the Elwoods had anything to do with it. But their back door, through which the robber must have entered, was readily visible from the Elwoods' yard, and they hoped one of the children might have seen—well, a tramp maybe—slip in and out with the loot.

John Elwood called his children together and lined them up for questioning. "Was any of you playing back there in the yard?''

"Hatcher was,'' one of the girls said. "He was playing out there by himself for an hour before supper.'' Hatcher often played, alone, games that involved pointless tracings in the ground and all kinds of silly mumbo-jumbo that he made up.

"Didn't you see anybody go in over there?" Elwood demanded a bit fiercely.

Hatcher smiled and shook his head.

"Let me look in your pockets, boy." Hatcher stepped forward and without expression let the pockets of his overalls be searched. His father found a pocket knife he didn't recognize, some odd-shaped pebbles, and what looked like the tin label from a plug of tobacco, a little glinting medallion. Nothing else.

"Hatcher, tell these folks if you know anything about it," Elwood said earnestly.

"Now don't rattle off at the boy," the neighbors said. "It's probably our fault anyway for not keeping the money in the bank."

"I don't want there to be any suspicion that any of mine did it."

"Certainly not," the neighbors affirmed. "It wasn't that we figured it that way at all. But you know how you feel when you lose money."

"I didn't see anyone go in your house," Hatcher said. His eyelids, transparently blue as those of a little chicken, dropped over his eyes and he gave them a smile of dismissal.

The next afternoon Mrs. Elwood got a call from the hardware store.

"Ma'am, your boy Hatcher is in here."

"Yes?"

"He wants to buy a gun."

"What? Wait a minute. I think there's something burning on the stove." She returned soon to say, "Wasn't anything burning I could find. I was sure I could smell it. What did you say?"

"Hatcher wants to...He has eighteen dollars and says he wants to buy a revolver—for his father he says—and the reason I'm calling you is that, like I told him, it would cost a little more than that, but I was wondering if you knew he had this money, a boy his age."

"Thank you," Mrs. Elwood said, her ordinarily small voice dwindling. "Don't sell him anything. Please tell him to come home. Right away."

The hardware clerk had made a natural but fatal miscalculation in leaving his counter to make the phone call. When he returned he discovered that Hatcher was gone—with the eighteen dollars, a Stevens .22 calibre revolver, and four boxes of shells. The clerk immediately called Mrs. Elwood again.

Somehow—perhaps by her natural sweetness, by Elwood's reputation for honesty, by virtue of her being still remembered after thirteen years as Marcus Hatcher's daugher—she persuaded the clerk to raise no alarm until her husband should have come home from work to give her counsel. "I'm sure we can straighten it out. Whatever it costs...." she said.

"I'm more worried what he might do with that gun," the clerk said. "A boy his age."

"Could he hurt himself?"

"That's not what I'm worried about either," the clerk said meanly.

When John Elwood came home and learned all he had to be told, he dropped on the porch steps and put his head in his hands for a while. He was very tired. At that time he was temporarily on a job of excavating a basement under an old house. He was used to heavy work and odd jobs—he had seldom had anything else. Nevertheless a day's work with a shovel beats down any man. To come home from that to be told that his seven-year-old son was a crime wave struck him as unjust, though he would not have worried at that time about who authored the injustice.

Presently he stood up straight and told his wife, "Call the kids." With them gathered around him at the foot of the porch steps he said, "Now you listen to me. I want you to go all over town and I don't want you *asking* where he is. I want you to find him. Look. Look in the trees and barns and outhouses—everywhere. If any of you tells a soul what's going on, I'll larrup you so you'll remember, I promise. I don't think the whole town needs to know what's going on."

With the children dispatched like faithful guerrillas, Elwood and his wife set out fast for the business district of town, the block and a half of stores, barber shops, gas stations, and beer parlors where at this hour the most curious and potentially talkative townspeople would be gathered. Elwood broke into a trot, and his frail wife trotted behind him like a ripped and dangling banner at the stern of a beat-up ship.

They had absolutely no good luck with Hatcher. By the time they hit the business district they were too late. A crowd was gathered beside the bank, where an outside stairway led up to Dr. Hill's office. Vivian Elwood cried out a little squeak of fright.

"He's not hurt," her husband said grimly, as though some accurate pessimism had elevated him to clairvoyance.

They were met in the center of the street by Dr. Hill who detached himself from the crowd like a hysterical centipede, gesturing and dancing with more arms and legs than they had ever seen on a human being. "Your kid," he said. "*He* is in my office. I looked up and he's pointing this gun right between my eyes."

"All right," Elwood said in a hangdog voice.

"Yes," the doctor hissed triumphantly. "It's all right if he wrecks everything and gets into God knows what drugs and poison, specimens, charts...."

"I'll fetch him," Elwood said. "Be quiet."

"We could call the county seat and have the sheriff bring tear gas," someone in the crowd suggested.

"In my office?" Dr. Hill said. "Let Elwood think of a way to get him out."

"Hush," Elwood said. "I'll fetch him."

Perhaps it was not a heroic spectacle he made, climbing those iron stairs of the outside stairway. After all, people thought later, it wasn't as though there were a desperado up there, or he the lonely sheriff going up to bring the outlaw to justice. It was only his own queer son.

But anyway the people in the crowd got some momentary feeling that his climb was the act of a brave man; maybe at least the act of a man walking stiffly through his own humiliation. They saw the uneven stain of sweated salt on his shirt, and they remembered that he was always a hard-working and dependable man who deserved some moral support.

After he'd been in the office ten minutes and came down leading Hatcher, looking at no one, the crowd parted with a certain respect. Only Dr. Hill had any questions.

"He didn't touch your stuff," Elwood said. "That wasn't what he was after." Then brusquely he said to his wife, "Come home." Everyone had to make up from his own imagination the scene in the doctor's office and to guess what Hatcher had wanted there.

They did this liberally, and also imagined the kind of licking Hatcher would get. So no one was really cheated of an opportunity to enjoy the episode. All summer long people were talking about it and laughing. But what had Hatcher wanted at Dr. Hill's? It seemed an odd place for him to go.

Of course in reality Hatcher did get a brutal whipping that night. His father laid on with his belt wickedly, and there was no nonsense spoken about the whipping hurting him worse than it did the boy. Elwood was a simple enough man to believe that punishment isn't given or withheld by whim. It follows certain acts for boys or men, and each of them has to take what's coming.

When he had finished the whipping, he rolled down his sleeves and said to the wailing boy, "It's done with now. Just remember to keep away from what doesn't belong to you, hear?''

The boy nodded and through his tears a little smirk appeared—not intentionally, one supposes, but as the natural contraction of his face in the aftermath of pain.

What Elwood bore as a result of the crimes was a certain coldness from the neighbors across the garden, the settlement of three dollars to the hardware store, and a certain amount of tiresome joshing from the men he worked with or met on the street. He knew that all his children were getting the same mockery, and he figured they could all stiffen their backs and wait for it to die away.

Before it had a chance to, Hatcher was in bad trouble again. This time he caught a three-year-old girl in the alley behind her home, roped her to a fence, piled brush around her, and set fire to it. Fortunately the girl's mother heard her screaming and arrived in time to save her from real injury. But—''the child could have been killed'' and the child did have bad dreams that went on and on with no sign of diminishing.

The town was watching, and for the coarser element this attempt of Hatcher's was again a laughing matter, though even this laughter now had something of the incredulous in it. At the pool hall you would hear men joking about it who, in the midst of a peal of laughter, might pause with their mouths open and a quizzical look in their eyes like embarrassment. It was from this time that some of the older boys in town invented the nickname Hatchet—or The Hatchet— which everyone heard of and more or less accepted, even those thoughtful ones who were sympathetically concerned about the boy.

A group composed of the Methodist minister, Hatcher's schoolteacher, the town mayor, and the mother of the little girl called on the Elwoods. They sat in the Elwood parlor with their problem, slightly constrained, friendly, insistent.

"You see, John and Virginia," the minister said, "we understand too that children are children and that they do unpredictable things at times. We understand too that disciplining Hatcher is your problem. But...."

"I gave him a good licking," Elwood said. "You know I'd do that. And I'm awfully sorry about the little girl."

"She wasn't really hurt," Virginia Elwood suggested. She looked around the circle of earnest, faintly hostile eyes and tittered. "Are you people sure you won't have some lemonade? Or coffee?"

"Perhaps a licking isn't what the boy needed," the minister said.

Hatcher's teacher nodded enthusiastic agreement. "I've come to the conclusion that there are no problem children, only problem par...."

"Yes," the minister interrupted her. But whether Elwood recognized the maxim she was quoting or not, he caught the drift of her thought. He said reflectively, "But the others are all fine kids. We've treated them all the same. I don't understand it."

"None of us pretends to. *Fully. Yet,*" the minister said. "Our thought was simply that here might be an occasion when we should call on outside help."

"I've prayed," Elwood said, blushing and shifting his feet.

The minister coughed into his handkerchief. "We meant that it might be wise to ask the opinion of the county health authorities. They've had experience and training with special children."

The mayor, who was a kind old man with a voice so harsh that he hated to talk much, broke in. "People's scared, John. That's the sad truth. They're scared for their children and things. It's nothing against you folks or the rest of your kids."

Elwood nodded, stood up, and yawned in their faces. The ladies of the delegation interpreted this later as an affront, but the mayor held the opinion that it more probably indicated fatigue of the mind that made Elwood behave as he would not ordinarily.

"No," Elwood said. "Thank you all. But no."

"Something's got to be done," the mayor said.

Elwood agreed. "It will be, by God, if I have to put a collar on him and hook him to a clothesline."

The teacher lifted her hand in a delicate appeal. "That's not the way."

"Don't you worry. I'll put the other boys onto him and there won't be any more trouble from him ever. I promise that. Is that enough for you?"

So, through the rest of that summer no one ever saw Hatcher by himself. His three older brothers took turns shepherding him and the other children spied. If there were lots of times when they all wanted to turn their backs on him and flee, still there is a general agreement that they did a remarkable job of guarding him; and their efficiency is a testimony to the family discipline and loyalty that Elwood inspired. None of them liked Hatcher any more. You could tell that for them he had been recognized as a foreigner—their brother, but an intruder, as strangely altered to them as if their own hands might turn overnight into biting and loathsome rodents. They did their careful duty to him.

Until one evening his next-older brother, Tommy, brought him into the yard bleeding from the nose and from cuts around his mouth. Tommy was pale and shaking so that it was hard for him to talk. He led Hatcher through the front gate and stood unhappily beside him until Elwood looked up from his evening paper and summoned them to the porch.

"What'd he do and who beat him up?"

"Me," Tommy said.

"You beat him up? What was he trying to do?"

"Nothing," Tommy said. "He made me bust the ME church window and then I let him have it."

Elwood licked his lips. This was the kind of excuse that would have made him laugh a few months before, and he would have had a ready, hard answer for it. He wasn't so sure any more.

"How could he *make* you do it?"

"I don't know, Dad. We were walking back from the ball diamond. Mickey Alfred's guys went out to practice this afternoon and we was watching them. So we came by the church...."

"Did he dare you to do it?"

"Dad, I don't think so, but I don't know."

"You can't tell me," Elwood said, less in irony than as the registration of a fact that he would blindly and unwillingly accept. "Go in the house, Tommy. You didn't have to beat him up quite so bad."

He pushed forward in the porch swing and beckoned Hatcher. The boy, as usual through these hot days, was dressed in a single garment of bib overalls faded to a chalky blue. His skin was pale as milk gravy. For some reason he would never tan no matter how much time he passed in the sun. His wrist lay slender as an axe handle inside the work-grimed fingers his father reached to hold him.

"What's the trouble, old sport?" Elwood asked.

"Nothing, Dad." Hatcher tried to twist himself free of the hand tightening on his wrist. "I'm all right." His little blue eyes darted here and there like those of a weasel seeking escape.

"Why do you do these mean things?" his father coaxed. "You don't like this old town, I guess. Maybe we ought to move out of here and start over again somewhere else."

"I like it," Hatcher said.

Elwood studied the small face as he never had before. Perhaps in studying it he was trying to puzzle out all the things that had gone wrong without obvious cause in his own life, the failures that reason couldn't account for.

Maybe he was remembering the time he had married Virginia, when his confidence had been strong because he knew he could work as hard as any man and believed that at least a decent success would follow from that. Old man Hatcher would have to admit some day that he had been wrong to oppose their marriage. It seemed to him nothing but bad luck that things had not yet turned out that way. Maybe he believed that his son was running in a similar streak of bad luck that would have to turn soon.

"You and me," he said to the boy sentimentally. "You and me, we should cut out of this town together and find a better one."

Hatcher did not look at him. The boy was licking some dried blood from his cheek, evidently enjoying the taste. "I like it here, Dad," he said.

That night the deputation consisting of the mayor, the minister, and the teacher came again. They were certain that it was Hatcher who had broken the window. The mayor said, "The neighbors seen, John. It was Hatcher."

"Did they see him throw the rock? *Which* one of them seen it?"

He made them admit that they had only hearsay evidence. No one had actually seen the stone fly from Hatcher's hand, but wasn't it probably...?

"To hell with that talk," Elwood said. "Tommy told me he did it. Tommy wouldn't lie."

"There's no need for you or Tommy to protect Hatcher," the minister said.

"It wasn't Hatcher."

They took his word for it finally, but they said the next time there was trouble they would call the county authorities without consulting him. The mayor said, "I'm sorry, John," as he shook hands. Elwood knew that they were serious about their threat.

After them, on the same evening, old Marcus Hatcher came. He had not been in their house for nearly eight years—he had been obliged to make the last visit by the death of one of their little girls.

Marcus Hatcher was a man who would pass for a great figure in this community. He had built up a holding of several farms, had served in the state legislature, and now lived in partial isolation in a big house in the country. His other daughters, who had married better than Virginia, lived in scattered cities throughout the state and he spent a good deal of time in visiting them. Yet this was his town. He had conquered it once as a young man, and he held it yet like a partially liberated province. The chances are that he had been informed of all little Hatcher's crimes and had been gathering rage for this visit.

He came in without knocking. He rapped on the parlor floor with his cane and when his daughter and son-in-law looked to see who was there, he delivered his point shortly.

"Get rid of that boy."

"Come sit down, Daddy," Virginia said. "We can talk quieter if we're all comfortable."

The old man allowed her to push up a chair behind him. He dropped into it grudgingly. "You named him after me. Hatcher. I should have protested at the time. Now look. Whenever anyone says Hatcher they mean that monster, that pirate."

"I reckon we named him Hatcher because Virginia was fond of you," Elwood said. "There was no thought of giving you shame."

"Hatcher's not a bad boy," Virginia said. "His teacher thinks he may be what they call a psychopathic personality."

"Be damned," old man Hatcher said. "I'm giving you good advice. Get rid of that boy. Give him to the reform school."

"I don't know why we should," Elwood said.

"He's worthless. Deny that."

"I won't deny it, but he's ours and I'll manage him."

Virginia broke into tears and in the midst of them her father departed. When he was gone she said brokenly, "What *will* we do with the boy? We've tried everything. We've whipped him and been kind to him."

"It wasn't him that broke the window." But this argument seemed to have lost its sinew, and Elwood let it float away. "Maybe we haven't done enough of either."

From that time on he tried both kindness and punishment like a daily hygienic practice, intensely, as though he imagined that the real person of his son was sleeping somewhere inside the shell they knew, and still required to be wakened by more vigorous summons—kind actions and the belt.

There were times when he would finish talking to Hatcher when the sweat of disgust with himself would be blinding him and times when he finished whipping the boy—for nothing much—when he would find himself really sick, with his legs trembling and his stomach squeezing in and out. Then he would pray.

He used sometimes to go into the woodshed and fling himself on the pile of coal and grovel and whine in his need for some guidance or justification, and he got no light.

72

At the commencement of the fall term the Elwoods kept Hatcher out of school. The school principal demanded no explanation, though here was an infraction of the compulsory education law. It was as though everyone agreed that Hatcher was getting ready for new crimes and that it was better for them not to happen around school.

At the school there was a memory of many unexplained misdemeanors and bits of nastiness—the home economics class had found a toad floating in a kettle of grape juice once, someone had set fire to the Fourth Grade's Christmas tree and burned all the little presents under it, a chicken's entrails had been found in Miss Halvorsen's coat pocket—all this in recent years. No one would say flatly that Hatcher had done all these things, but they were the kind of thing now expected of him.

But his last crime was simply too subtle for their comprehension. His own hands had no part in it.

On October 31st, a day long to be remembered in the town, the banker opened his vault in the morning to find a big hole in the top of it. The hole led up through the floor of Dr. Hill's office. Dr. Hill had skipped town and with him had gone thirteen thousand dollars' worth of green and negotiable paper.

The town was shocked and shamed. This was worse than a death. People had loved Dr. Hill—or they had convinced themselves that they must love him, since he knew so much about most of them, things they wouldn't want known by people they didn't love.

All day little flurries of shocked comment whipped through town like the snowsprays of a killing blizzard. Schoolchildren, neighbors, the hangers-on at the pool halls, all talked of the theft in terms of fright and shock. Deposits were insured, of course, but what could one count on if a man of Dr. Hill's prosperity, his long and devoted service, his domestic contentment, and his intelligence could break down and commit a sneaky crime?

John Elwood was as shocked as the rest. All day long while he shoveled grain at the elevator—and at noon when he ate his lunch alone, sitting by a half-filled box car and glaring at the gray, empty sky—he kept thinking what a shame it was that Dr. Hill had been tempted in this devilish way.

When all his kids were in bed that evening, he told his wife he thought he'd go up town a little while to hear if there was any news. He might have one beer, he said, to cheer himself up a little. Virginia didn't worry about this at all. She knew that John was a very temperate man with alcohol.

There wasn't any news. There weren't even many people in the pool hall where he went for his beer. Of course Rick Henline was there, with the rumor that the state police had cornered Dr. Hill and shot him down in a corn field near Oskaloosa. But Otell Jowett and his cousin Frank, who had been listening to recent radio reports, were in a position to refute this. No one was there to offer another theory.

Otell said to Elwood jokingly, "Seems like that kid of yourn would have done everybody a favor if he'd shot the Doc last summer when he went after him."

"What?" Elwood screeched, jerking himself alert from his brooding. "What do you mean he *went after him?*"

"Why, when he took his gun and...."

"My kid had nothing to do with this devilment," Elwood said.

"For the Lord's sake, man," Otell explained to him. "I didn't aim to say he had. Why should I think a thing like that?"

Elwood's eyes were rolling wildly. "People want to blame everything on that boy," he said. "You'd think he was the devil himself the way this town tries to blame him for everything."

The few drinkers in the pool hall stared at John Elwood as though he had finally popped his lid. They stared—and saw him catch himself as though a great, simple truth had suddenly come to him. They saw him fumble like a blind man for his sheepskin coat and march without another word into the whistling night.

When he was gone they asked each other how many beers he'd had to make him flake up so unpredictably, and after a bit they were all convinced that it was at least twelve.

Elwood found his wife in the kitchen. Nothing unusual about that; she had spent most of her time on earth there. But she said later that he acted very much surprised to see her as he came in the back door. Surprised and upset and generally—well, just funny.

"Where are the kids?" he asked.

"Why they're all asleep."

"Hatcher?"

"He's asleep too. I think he may be coming down with the grippe. He called me a while ago. He had some fever and threw up. I took him into our room and put him in our bed so's he wouldn't disturb the others."

"In our bed?" Elwood asked. Then he shivered, his wife told later. "So he's in our bed now?"

"Why, he's been there before," Virginia said mildly. "I don't understand why you should take on about that." She poked at the coals in the stove and a puff of black smoke flashed up through the top of the stove and vanished in the kitchen's shadows.

"Don't you come up," Elwood said to her menacingly. And the way he said it finally showed her that there was something wrong in his mind, that there was something terrible bothering him. She couldn't think what he meant to do. She tried to follow him when he climbed the stairs to the bedroom, clutching at his arm and crying for him to explain what he wanted with Hatcher. Roughly he shoved her back. He went into the room where the sick child was sleeping and locked the door behind him.

Before he even looked at Hatcher he went to the dresser and took his razor from the top drawer. He unfolded the blade, turning to the bed. The blade flickered close to Hatcher's ear, close to the artery ticking in the boy's throat. Some light came into the room from a nearby street lamp. There was no other illumination.

"Hatcher," Elwood whispered.

His only answer was the quick breathing of a child in a fever dream. He could smell the bile that had risen a while before when his son's body had been shaken with the purifying convulsions of its disease.

Again he brought the razor close to the boy's throat. He tried to pray for strength to finish what he had begun. His prayer was blocked in his gullet. He could not pray for help in killing his own son. All right, he would do it without prayer. But his courage was not quite great enough to do it while the boy slept. There had to be some kind of communication or it would be like killing an innocent stranger.

"It was you, after all," Elwood whispered. "It *was* you that broke the church window and tempted the Doc. I don't know how you done it, but you done it. I'm going to send you back to hell."

The boy woke and rolled feverishly on his pillow. He coughed with an effort. "M' stomick hurts," he wailed pitifully.

"What, son?"

"Daddy, Daddy...."

With an awful groan Elwood threw his razor against the wall. The boy's waking plea had jolted him back to a human realization of what he had been about to do. Elwood *knew*...and ran out of the house like an animal that feels its body start to respond to a poison it has swallowed.

He ran first to the house of the Methodist minister and frightened that poor man terribly by battering his way through the front door and then by telling the wildest story—or delusion—the minister had ever heard.

It was Elwood's belief, fear, or hallucination, the minister said, that he had found an actual devil inhabiting the boy Hatcher. Not just the spirit of mischief or "devilment," in which the minister admitted that he himself could believe, but something at least as substantial and effective as a disease. Like those viruses we hear about, only a lot more nimble. For Elwood claimed that the devil had jumped from the boy right to him, and he bellowed, "It was the devil that put that razor in my hand."

Maybe because Elwood did not think he had time to tell the story fully, the minister did not understand his allusion to the razor. Being modern in his views, he took no stock in Elwood's frantic plea for help in getting the devil, which had jumped from Hatcher, out of himself. At the same time, the minister wanted to help Elwood to calm himself. When he told of it later, the minister said that he suggested they go call on Doc Hill to ask for a sedative. He suggested this before he remembered what had happened to the Doc. But anyway his suggestion set Elwood off.

Elwood began to laugh, then, in a way that made the minister's blood run cold. He laughed and shouted, "Yeah, I'll go see the Doc." Then he turned on his heel and stomped out. He had come, the minister said, sick as a poisoned dog, but he left rampaging like a buck sheep.

Back uptown Elwood saw Otell Jowett getting into his car. He ran at Otell with his head lowered and butted Otell's wind out. He took Otell's car. And that was strictly the last anyone in our town ever saw of him.

The police found Otell's car up near the state capital the next morning, off the road and burned right down to the steel, but there was no sign of Elwood. Everyone thought he'd wrecked the car while he was still out of his mind and had just kept on running.

Afterward? Why, afterward it turned out that his desertion was not altogether inconvenient, even if most people condemned it. Old Marcus Hatcher stopped being so vindictive and stingy with the family. He settled some money on Virginia and persuaded her to send two of the older boys to live with a sister in a bigger town where they had more chance to make something of themselves. The other kids got better clothes for school and Sunday. The old man even arranged for Hatcher to be sent to a famous Boy's Republic in another state, where, from all reports, he grew up to be a fine young man, likely to be useful to his country.

In a few years Hatcher's escapades and his father's desertion were almost dropped from the town's habitual conversation. There had been those who predicted Elwood would come back. He had always been a good father and he had loved his family as much or more than the next one. He had always been a sober, reasonable man except for his last, beery fling. And they reasoned that a man can't hold out forever against what he feels for his kids.

But he didn't come, so the town said, "There's more to it than we know," and let it go at that. In the absence of a more definite epitaph they agreed complacently with his wife's cryptic dismissal—"I think John let it get him finally."

The Gadfly

Blinking from the brightness of the April day, leading six young Matchlocks burdened like porters on safari, Fidelity Matchlock came into her kitchen after her weekly trip to the A&P to find her oldest daughter, Juliet, waiting with the bad news.

"Listen!" Juliet commanded, and promptly reset her mouth in a smile of cynicism that had been maturing for all of her thirteen years.

Still holding a pack of Cokes in her right hand, Fidelity brushed a sweated strand of hair from her forehead with her right wrist. "Finch, don't put the rolls in the sink. Potatoes out in the pantry, please! Margarita, *can't* you hold the screen until Philippe gets through? Philippe, if you'd *let* me tie your shoe...Darling, how can I hear anything above this din? Now then, what is it I'm supposed to listen to?"

Juliet only jerked her head toward the open door of the stairway that led up to the innocent, cluttered bedrooms of the second floor— and on up to the attic study where Prof. Harold Graber Matchlock habitually barricaded himself to grade student themes and prepare his lectures in English History.

"Finch!" Fidelity dragged the bread box open with the toe of her shoe and elbowed her second son until he dropped the package of hamburger rolls into it. Then, after the screen door banged and the clatter of catsup bottles and milk bottles subsided as her children settled their burdens on floor and table and freezer, she could hear something.

"Well," she said with a motherly wink for the relentless frown-above-the-smile on Juliet's pretty face. "Well, Daddy came home from the campus early today, didn't he?"

In the relative silence the sound of a hard-hit typewriter came down the stairs. It rattled insistently above early spring bird calls, above the whisper of wind in the elms, and the mellow barking of Dr. Patchen's spaniel across the street. The machine was being hammered at such a reckless pace that its very tempo communicated indignation. Fidelity thought in her first moment of dizziness, despair, and recognition that the last machine gun of a beleaguered garrison would sound like this before the human tides rolled over it.

"He's writing the letter," Juliet said. "He's writing it *anyway*." Which meant that little pitchers certainly did have big ears, and that Juliet understood exactly what crisis had been brewing since the big thaw in March.

For over three weeks now Harold's indignation had been swelling. He was, admittedly, slow to anger; the deliberate pace of his angering produced a heavier head of steam. This time he had not been directly involved in conflict. He was merely an interested faculty bystander when the student editors of the college literary magazine put themselves in opposition to the administration of Minota College. The connection had to do with some obscene words in a story and a poem that had, by now, been printed in the spring issue of *The Redbird*. The Administration had got wind of the offense before type was set, had objected and shilly-shallied, and now was holding up distribution of the printed copies. From the beginning Harold had been sympathetic with the Administration's quandary. And yet—and *yet!*—what ultimate right had they to forbid the publication of the offending student works? The weaseling, hypocritical denials of intolerance had stuck in Harold's craw. In his discussions of it with Fidelity—these almost nightly affairs in the last week—Harold had begun to insist he must write a blistering letter of protest to President Grace.

Juliet, if not the other children, must have been listening from the head of the stairs or at the laundry chute. No use to quibble that Juliet

82

was too young to grasp her father's fine points on the old enigma of censorship. It was enough to hope she was too young to understand the words in the magazine Harold had brought home, in the not impossible event that she had hunted it out of his papers.

Juliet had understood enough to be sure now that her father was in the attic preparing his challenge...*against any person or persons whatsoever, so help me God*...He was up there calling dear old President Grace a "censorious tyrant." He was probably back to his old tactic of threatening "instant resignation" unless the Administration saw the light of his truth. And Juliet could understand as well as her mother this meant that once again the Matchlock family would have to look for a new job in a new town.

Fidelity said, "All right now, you children. You help Juliet put everything away. Get the ice cream in the freezer first, darling. Put the bananas in the fruit basket. I want to talk to your father for a few minutes."

She could not believe that Harold heard her climb up to his study in the attic. The warlike chattering of the typewriter did not slacken even when she tried the doorknob. After she knocked there was only a tiny pause, then a particularly sharp rush of keys as he finished a sentence.

"Sweetie? Sweetie? It's so warm out today. The children wanted me to ask if you'd come down and have ice cream and bananas with them, after...May I come in, sweetheart?"

She hadn't really thought that oblique approach would work. Slow to anger, Harold had come to such a flood of indignation that nothing short of cannonfire could make him hear. She could imagine him in there hunched over the typewriter like a gunner in the lull of battle, sweat gleaming from his hair and mustache, his eyes narrowed to the frame of the ribbon holder on his machine as to the aperture of a gunsight.

"Sweetheart, if you're writing to President Grace...." She knew he was; she was afraid her pretense of ignorance would only stiffen him in his resolve. Nobody could fool Harold. Alas...! "If you're writing him, don't forget what you said last night. You said he's probably just as eager as anyone else to find some way to compromise this dispute with the student magazine."

For reply the typewriter was hit twenty-one strokes, including three strokes on the space bar. Apparently her plea had done nothing more than suggest a pithy wording for him to use in his letter.

"Darling," she said meekly, "I don't mean to bother you while you're deep in thought. I'll go away if you'll just promise to let me read the letter before you mail it. I won't even say anything to you about it, not even *discuss*. Please. I only want to get the exact wording in my mind so I'll be prep—...."

Wham, wham, wham, SOCK. At full volume the first notes of Beethoven's Fifth Symphony came through the attic door like a fist in a comic strip scene, punching her right in the faithful schnozzle.

He had blasted her with Beethoven from his portable machine, put up there ostensibly to lull him with soft airs while he labored. This blast of music was his only reply to her for all her years of not only following him when he threw away job after job by defying college administrations, but for all her efforts in justifying him to people. It was she, not he, who had to explain to his puzzled father and mother why a young man who'd started out as brilliantly as Harold from graduate school had descended, in ten years of diligent work, the academic ladder with such precipitous steps. He had begun with a promising job at the U of Illinois. With four progressively less distinguished colleges in between he had now come to Minota College, Minota, Missouri. She had put a good face on these moves to her parents, and to her children as they each, in turn, reached the age of reason and required to know why each new set of pets and friends had to be bid goodbye so soon as the Matchlocks made their pilgrimage from one college town to another.

"Harold!" she screamed. But he was drowning out her voice with a reminder that in his passion he owed no loyalty to anything but the great soldierly swell of music. Within the week, she remembered, she had heard him playing the same record downstairs and explaining to Finch, Robert, Philippe, and Susan that at the beginning of World War II the Warsaw radio station had played this music as its theme until the screaming Stukas silenced it. He made their eyes shine like his own by telling how the Polish cavalry had formed in colorful battle array and actually charged in resplendent hopelessness against Hitler's ugly black tanks in their grain fields. "Harold, I hate censorship as much as you do," she shrieked at the door. 'Harold, we're not the Polish cavalry. We're...."

It was no use. But she still hoped to slow him down until his fury began to simmer down. Until that dreadful music stopped. If she could actually get the letter in her hands and discuss it as a document—maybe praise him for its forcefulness and style, its allusions to great historical precedents—then there was a chance he might rewrite it, at least, before he mailed it. If he rewrote it, there was a chance he might omit any man-to-man defiance of President Grace and Dean Thresher for their part in the censorship squabble. If the personal defiance was left out, then they might not *have* to fire him, as, she ruefully admitted, the heads of Montana, Iowa State Teachers, South Dakota State and Warfield College had been forced to do. His favorite method of attack was to lay his head on the block and dare them to cut it off.

At the bottom of the stairs all seven of her children were clustered. Their eyes, watching her descend in retreat, looked already hungry. They silently reminded her of what she knew too well—that a hurried exit from Minota College meant the end of Harold's academic career.

"Juliet," she said, "honey, you take Margarita and Susan up to play in the stairs outside his door. When he comes out, be real nice to him. Tell him what you did today and all that kind of thing."

"He's even got stamps to mail it with," Juliet said. "He took them from your desk while you were shopping. I saw him."

"Yes," Fidelity said, "and, Robert, you and Finch and Philippe and Tommy play out on the porch or sidewalk and when he comes down you might tell him that Mama would like a word with him before he goes anywhere."

In the kitchen she busied herself putting away the rest of the groceries. Usually her children did a better job than they had this time. From the minute Juliet had confronted them with her news of trouble they had flipped away the veneer of discipline. Now each of them had to trust, just as she did, that panic itself would show them how to cope with the uncertainty that had fallen upon them.

As she worked, Fidelity listened for the cessation of the typewriter's rattle—and the strain of listening only made her more sensitive and receptive to the music he had turned on her. Thus, in spite of her fears she felt her spine stiffen and her chin lift. Oh, this music was titanic and wonderful, all right, with a warrior beauty, like old flags going by, and it made her feel beautiful inside as no bodily sensation could. That was how music tricked you, she thought. Harold meant to trick her with it, but most of all he was tricking himself. Nobody could fool him, but the music always did. He took Beethoven's passion as a commandment directed to him personally. And so he would throw away all he deserved for being such a good teacher, a good father, a good man.

Don't *let* the music fool you, Harold! She would put it to him just like that when he came down. And if she could get a smile out of him at this brusque absurdity her battle was halfway won. She only had to make him proceed gently. They liked him here at Minota. President

Grace practically gaped whenever her good man spoke at faculty meetings. Dean Thresher had openly admitted in January that Harold's publications and grad school record were more distinguished than those of anyone else on the faculty.

"Mother," Juliet said tonelessly behind her. There she stood again, shrugging her worldly wisdom, utterly resigned. "Mother, he went down the rainspout."

"Down...?"

"He climbed down outside the house. He knew we were waiting for him. He saw we had the stairs roped off with bedsheets."

"You shouldn't have," Fidelity said.

"Don't cry, Mama," Juliet told her. "No use crying now. After all, you married the jerk."

The last hope died hard. "Tell the boys to run...."

"It's no use," Juliet said. "When we spotted him he was already through the hedge and going fast. He's made it to the mailbox already." She turned slowly, as if already on her way to say goodbye to their rabbit Hector and the silly little Patchen boy who claimed they were going steady because they so often watched television together.

Alone again in her kitchen, Fidelity kept on crying. She laid her head on the kitchen table until a sudden awful thought made her sit bolt upright. Swiftly she began to count backward through April and March. Each time before when Harold had fought it out with a college administration he had simultaneously got her pregnant. Finch at Illinois. Susan at Montana. Margarita at South Dakota State; little Philippe conceived in the spring he had defied the Warfield College administration for slackness in desegregating the one social sorority on its sorry campus. Had he done it again now?

She could not be sure. It was too soon to be sure of any such thing. But in her misery she was ready to believe that the whole pattern would be repeated. She buried her head in her arms and tried to think of the most sorrowful name for a baby girl, the most sorrowful for a baby boy. Deirdre of the Sorrows seemed to fall short. Job was somehow not enough. Call the boy Harold Graber Jr. Call the girl Fidelity.

His jet black hair parted in the middle and his heavy, jet black mustache made Harold Graber Matchlock look like a gunfighter—like one of the marshals of Dodge City or Abilene, a successor to, or maybe a predecessor, of Wild Bill Hickok, Bat Masterson or Doc Holliday. His piercing eyes were wrinkled at the corners as though he were always walking down the sunswept street of Tombstone at high noon. And he stood just a little short of five feet four inches.

Children, especially his own, adored him not merely because he looked like a character out of the Wild West, but because he was built on a scale to be a playmate of theirs. Some of this spontaneous love and trust carried over among the students wherever he taught. It was as though they, too, in their passage from childhood, recognized him as a proper champion against the injustices of the adult world. Everywhere he acquired a following, not only from students in his department, but from their buddies in English, Philosophy and Political Science.

He had the gift or curse of instant intimacy with the young. That was the source of all his trouble. By temperament and intellectual conviction he was a middle-of-the-roader. His doctoral thesis—subsequently revised and published in both England and the US under the title *Milton and the Roundheads*—soberly measured the consequences of Milton's libertarian rhetoric in the excesses committed by Cromwell's fanatic legions. The various deans and faculty selection committees who read his other published articles expected to hire a man who would stand for common sense give and take in departmental issues.

And—in departmental issues—they found him mild and temperate. But from the first he had been a sucker for student causes. The trouble had begun at Illinois over something as petty as dormitory hours for upper-class women. Probably when the first small group of devoted students lingered after class on that long ago day—it was in the spring; these debauches of rebellion always began in springtime— to argue whether young women should be tucked in bed like children at eleven, Harold had taken the Administration's side.

Yes, probably. But after the students had talked him into going with them for a meeting with the Illinois deans he had come home to tell Fidelity, "They are lying to the students." How well she had learned since then to recognize that deadly growl in his voice when he spoke of administrative lies! In his mind the dishonesty of the dealings superseded the surface issues. "What the administration wants is all right. They want it for the wrong reasons," he said. The Dean of Women and the Dean for Student Affairs had been on the verge of outwitting the students. Well, they could not fool him!

On that occasion at Illinois Fidelity had made the lighthearted mistake of pointing out that, in the interest of efficiency, administrations probably always doctored the truth before they spread it abroad through the student body. Plato's necessary lies, you know.

His mustache, already thick and black in those days, suddenly looked like a visor drawn down in preparation for combat. "Yes," he said with ominous quiet, "they probably always do."

87

So always and everywhere that he taught in the following years there had been a handy reason for him to lead the mutinies of righteous students.

"But Harold," Fidelity had pleaded once, "isn't there some way of registering dissent without resigning on the spot?" She came to know his single answer. He didn't want compromise because he saw that administrative compromises were always dictated by expediency. He would not have got involved in the first place except to vindicate inflexible principles.

"You never can," she said. And sometime—she thought it was after the fiasco at South Dakota State—he admitted she might be right. "And we've given so many hostages to fortune," she said in loving remonstrance.

"Ah," he retorted. "I used to think in graduate school, before Juliet was born, that I'd lose whatever gumption I had when we got children. For me it works the other way around. It's *because* of them I've got to. I only have courage for their sake."

Apparently. For at South Dakota State when he had just made her pregnant with Margarita, he got into the most unlikely squabble of all. Their English Department had inadvertently hired a mad hipster that year as an instructor of Freshman Composition and Survey of Modern Lit. The fellow not only began to preach the wholesome effects of marijuana and hallucinating drugs to his freshmen, he gained a student following by staging marijuana parties on the open prairie. He put *Lolita, The Tropic of Cancer, Lady Chatterly's Lover,* and *Naked Lunch* on the freshman reading list. When questioned about his pedagogic intents and advised to resign, he countered by organizing a student rally, complete with flaming torches and television coverage, in favor of academic freedom.

"Harold, you can't defend that man," Fidelity said, already admitting that it was not the hipster Harold meant to defend. It was the *principle*—however debauched, distorted, misrepresented, corrupted or mislaid. The principle was there and Harold would buckle on his invisible gunbelt and go into the street to fight for it. He pointed out, as he had pointed out to her before and would again, that he was not the only faculty member rising to the defense of their exotic colleague and his band of loyal students.

"But you're the only one who actually resigned when they wouldn't reinstate him," she cried later.

"Well," said Harold, squirming and blushing and obviously sorry the rest of the family had to pay for his decision, "well, it doesn't seem quite right to make a noise unless you're prepared to back it up *all the way*. Don't cry, Sweetie. I've already had a tenative offer from a Junior College in Utah.''

So it had gone on. Thus far they had barely avoided going to the Junior College level, though Harold had spent one year supervising a crew of unskilled laborers on a Federal dam in Montana until he could get another college job. Through the years he had moved his family from town to town in U-Haul trailers and rented trucks. He had uncomplainingly jimmied washing machines and their battered dryer up basement stairs from all the nice houses he had managed to find for them in so many college towns. He had caught new animals for the children to keep as pets. He had humiliated himself with dozens of real estate people. He had kept their old cars in repair with parts from Sears Roebuck. He had risen before countless dawns to work on scholarly articles that always appeared just in time to sway the balance and get him new jobs.

And she thought when they came by the skin of their teeth to the job at Minota College that maybe at last they might settle for a while, keep their family at its present size, and enjoy each other.

"It isn't us I'm worried about, you bastard ape," she had sung to him that day almost two years ago now when they sat among their dismantled furniture in this big, homely house five blocks from the Minota campus. "Don't you see it isn't the children and me I'm trying to make a home for? It's you. You deserve a rest."

She thought she had him then. He saw the pattern of their useless pilgrimage more sharply than she—after all, he was brighter, as the daddy is supposed to be. Put on his parole by their concern for him, he had absolutely and solemnly promised not to be drawn into *any* kind of controversy.

For eighteen months they had thrived. The students, as usual, loved him. The Matchlocks made friends among the faculty and townspeople as never before. Harold was at work on a new book, his first major publication since *Milton and the Roundheads*.

Then one March day, when the wind sang from the southwest and the clouds waved like huge white tulips in an ecstatic sky, a tall pockmarked student found his way to Harold's office. He had two manuscripts in his hand. He was the editor of *The Redbird*, Minota's occasional literary magazine.

"It isn't that I think these dirty words do the story any good. Or the poem either," he would have said to Harold.

"Ah. And you think they are offensive?"

"It isn't that I like to offend *anybody*," the boy said.

Of course, Harold might not have said a word of encouragement to him. The boy and the middle-aged man may just have sat on opposite sides of the desk waiting for truth to be made manifest. And then, probably, the boy would have noticed Harold watching his face. He would have caught the level, imperturbable look from those little black eyes under the gunfighter's brow. Noticing that look, the boy would have gulped and blinked. Then said, "It isn't the dirty words. It's the principle of the thing. So I've got to publish them."

No, it wouldn't have been Harold who mentioned principle. He had made a promise to Fidelity. It would have been the boy. But why was it in Harold's presence that the boy understood he absolutely "had to" wave his red cloth at the sleepy, tolerant administration of Minota College? Oh, it was a curse. Once upon a time Fidelity would have laughed at the idea of curses.

She couldn't any longer afford to laugh at anything. Her husband had found the one buried thread of justification for breaking his promise to her. And he had shinnied down the drainpipe with a letter in his teeth. He had once again challenged the whole world to act on principle or go for its gun.

She said, "I don't care if they burn every copy of that silly little magazine. I'd put a match to it myself."

But she looked around guiltily and then sighed with relief to find she was, truly, alone in her house and had not been overheard.

The night after Harold had mailed his ultimatum to President Grace he had shown her the carbon copy. While she read it he sat on their striped couch with his head hanging in pure sorrow. Of course he was ashamed of sliding down the rainspout like an escaping guerrilla at war with his own family. But he was not ashamed of the letter.

Nor was she, exactly. "It's beautiful," she said. "It's so...reasonable. I don't see how the Administration can possibly argue against your points. The way you bring in Milton...all that classic stuff...the bit about how tyrannies begin. Only...."

Only, why had he once again concluded his lovely document with a personal challenge, threatening them with instant resignation if they dreamed of further resistance to reason?

Harold nodded heavily to show he understood exactly what question she had left unspoken. But he might have answered—she almost wished he had—that it wouldn't have been beautiful without this last quixotic flourish. It might have been only academic windbaggery.

"Would you mail it tomorrow? That's all I want to ask?"

She thought he was going to die like a bushwhacked gunman. His jaw flexed and loosened awfully. His eyes rolled. He wouldn't answer. He just said, "It's *done*. I had to do it."

The next day she had an unmistakable attack of morning sickness. Gasping and gagging, she believed the whole, predictable future was announcing itself in her nausea. The Administration would *have* to fire him. She *was* pregnant. Poor President Grace, she thought with a sick laugh. He couldn't have guessed what he was getting when he got us.

But the doctor told her No. "Mrs. Matchlock, you're still a young woman and...ah...Mrs. Matchlock the symptoms would seem to indicate...ah...have you been under some, ah, severe emotional strain?"

She laughed in his face. He would never know what an emotional experience it was to watch Harold pace the living room floor quoting Sophocles, Milton, and Shelley.

The doctor murmured, "I don't want to insist, but I would strongly recommend that you see a friend of mine whose specialty is the psychiatric."

She looked the hypocrite right square in his professional eye and said slowly, "Doctor, I was made pregnant by five dirty words in the college literary magazine."

Then, having got exactly what she came for, she left him to struggle out of his amazement as best he could.

Nevertheless, it was putting things mildly to say she was relieved by the doctor's findings. She didn't mind being stark, staring crazy as long as she was not pregnant. For if she was not pregnant—that invariable sign—then surely the rest of her anxieties were part of a dream. The stamp had fallen off Harold's letter to the President. He had inadvertently addressed it to the President of the United States instead of the President of Minota College. The postman about to deliver it to President Grace's office in Old Main had been snatched from the sidewalk by an enormous bird and never heard from since. Surely, her superstition told her, some miracle had intervened. And this wild lightning burst of possibility made the whole city exult around her. Da, da, da, DAH! Wham, wham, wham, SOCK! These were the traffic sounds of downtown Minota, maybe. But, ah!, they were also the music of fate, just as Beethoven had written it.

When she came to her driveway at home she found it blocked by President Grace's Cadillac. The old gentleman was at ease on her striped couch, where Juliet had served him tea and a banana split. Fidelity interpreted his smile to mean that he hadn't a care in the world. But that, of course, was only his professional mask. He was here waiting for Harold, not for her. He had come, with relish, to fire Harold on the spot. To melt him down with brimstone there before the eyes of wife and children and to cast the residue into outer darkness.

President Grace always assumed the stance of a trapshooter when he shook hands. As he reached his immaculate hand across the coffee table to greet her, Fidelity closed her eyes and considered dragging him through the half-eaten banana split. He was a dear old glazed cookie, but he was Harold's enemy and she was Harold's wife.

"Your daughter and I have been having a lively discussion," President Grace told her, beaming and nodding his white head.

"About...?"

She saw it then, the ragged edge of Harold's fat letter protruding from the pocket of the old man's jacket. "Yes, about your problem," President Grace said.

"Juliet!"

"So I told him how Daddy *is*," Juliet said. Her eyes when she was being defiant squinched amazingly like her father's. "Sure, I told him how Daddy shinnied down the drainpipe and what he did in South Dakota and those other places. How he can't help writing these kind of letters. It's no worse than being an alcoholic. Or going to brothels like Professor Wheeler in Psych."

She had come home too late, Fidelity told herself faintly. The great wheels of disorder were spinning more wildly than seemed possible. "You mustn't say that about Professor Wheeler," she corrected faintly.

"You told Daddy that Dean Thresher's wife told you. Only you didn't say brothel. And those two Phys Ed instructors with short hair who live together, and...."

"He, he. We all have our faults," President Grace said. "But we're a happy college family anyway."

"And Daddy can't help himself when he gets in a state," Juliet said firmly—to either one or both of them. To whom it might concern. She was a very wise little girl, her mother realized.

Smiling in a manner that was getting harder and harder to interpret, President Grace pulled the letter from his pocket, drew the sheets from the envelope and began to read them again. From time to time he nodded approvingly. Then he said, "Your husband is a splendid writer, Mrs. Matchlock. If I weren't persuaded already, I feel he'd have the power to bring me one hundred and eighty degrees around to agree with him."

Very cautiously Fidelity said, "Agree? About the magazine? Then you're not going to censor it? You'll let it be pub—"

92

President Grace's beautiful hand waved like a silk handkerchief at the end of a magician's sleeve. "We burned the entire edition last weekend. No problem there. As I was saying...."

"You burned it?" Fidelity heard something like an echo sound faintly through the house. It was her own voice that had recently declared its unconcern if the magazine were burnt. Now that voice sounded ghastly strange to her. Aloud to President Grace she said, "You mean the students let you burn it? Wasn't there any...?" She meant to say "fight" but the word wouldn't come from her cold lips.

"Dean Thresher and I did it personally," the lovely old man told her. "It's one of the chores I've grown used to around Minota. Been here twenty-seven years now. Had to burn lots of student publications, though we're getting more tolerant with changing times. I've got it down to a science now. Can manage it very quietly. Sunday morning. That's the best time. Get the janitor to let us in to the editorial office. He helps us carry the junk over to the heating plant. Ffffft! As I was saying about your husband...."

"Didn't the students raise cain when they came Monday and found their magazine gone?"

President Grace winked at her. His tone was that of a generous father addressing his favorite daughter. "Ah, my dear. They're students. It's spring. They're rather relieved to be free for *other interests*. When they're told it all happened as a result of a misunderstanding on the janitor's part, my dear, they turn to more important matters. Now about this document your husband has written...."

Fidelity was still shaking her head in a daze when the President's graceful, subtle praise of Harold's *mind* and *power* and *integrity* turned the corner and approached his point.

"Gad," he was saying as she caught the line of his discourse, "it's exactly the kind of statement I need to use as a club on the Trustees. Marvelously stated! Overwhelming in its logic! Passionate! Unequivocating! If you can help me persuade your husband to change the wording just a little. Strike out these references to a magazine. That's no longer an issue. Fix it so the issue seems to be whether the Trustees will give us an appropriation for a new lab and classrooms. I can promise at least fifteen more faculty signatures to support his. And, though this is not to be thought of as in any sense connected, Dean Thresher and I are almost sure that a strong assault this spring on the Trustees will result in a nice boost in faculty salaries."

"Goody," said Juliet.

It would not be correct or fair to say that President Grace was bobbing up and down with excitement. Merely, the light of a greedy vision flowed from his face. The shine of his smile seemed to project the spires and campus green of such a college as no one had ever seen on this earth. It would be as delicate and tasty as spun sugar. He wanted that college with a pure hunger. What he wanted was surely good. Good Harold Matchlock could help him get it.

Now might be the time for wife and wise children to pitch in and strike a blow for academic affluence as well as their own happiness. That was what all three of them understood as they gazed at each other with uncertain smiles. Of course, of course, Fidelity thought. Of course we can get around Daddy in his present frame of mind....

"Mom's up in your study," Juliet said severely to her father. "She's typing a letter for you to sign."

Slowly, Harold Matchlock began to climb the stairs. It was five o'clock in the afternoon and he had just come from a conference with the student editor of *The Redbird*. It had been a most bewildering conference, beginning with a shock of suspicion and alarm when the boy told him how a janitor had burned the spring issue by mistake. The shock turned into paralyzed anger and at last into simple numbness when he realized that *nobody*—neither the rebellious authors nor their student supporters nor the editor himself—was much dismayed by the turn of events. "At least no one can say we backed down," the solemn youth declared. "They'll have to admit we stuck to our guns as long as there was any point in doing so."

Harold had no reply to this. When the boy left him alone in his office, he grunted once out loud, a tired, expiring grunt, then got his cap from the hook on the door and started home to face his family. Once again only Harold Matchlock was left holding the bag. The bag was full of stones, and with his letter to President Grace he had tied the stones around his own neck. Once again the kids and Fidelity would sink with him. For nothing.

His steps dragged on the campus walks. But the late afternoon was so beautiful it seemed like it was trying to tell him something—as if it had a secret that had been saved up for just such an occasion. Presently he found himself standing perfectly still, turned from the street and staring into the heart of a lilac bush beginning to bud. He could not remember halting, but there he was.

Staring, he realized what he was obliged to try. There might not be much chance to square things with President Grace at this late hour, but he had to make the gesture, had to throw down all his pride in an attempt to stave off the ultimate calamity.

He would prepare by shaving off his mustache—it was suddenly horribly clear to him that this black brush on his face had probably always been offensive to the Presidential eye. Clean-shaven, cap in hand, he must plead for tolerance. He would chuckle and smile to show what a fool he had been to fly off half-cocked—what a fool he still was, though a harmless one. Maybe he ought to take Fidelity and the children with him to testify he hadn't meant those adamant things he had written in his letter.

When this intent came clear in his mind, he felt an almost physical relief, as if a sweet breeze had begun to blow on his face. He foresaw that—*still*, if things broke right—he might make a decent, happy life for his family here at Minota. Do more things for the kids...for the little woman. Those good soldiers deserved a relief from the wars he had led them through.

He was ready to offer this vision to his wife when he opened the study door and saw her.

"Fidelity!"

She had a pencil in her teeth. Her blouse was unbuttoned. Loops of hair swirled on her damp forehead. He had never dreamed that the mother of his children could look quite so practical.

"Just a minute!" she growled at him. Her capable, strong hands poised above the typewriter keys. When she struck them, it was as if she were hurling a thunderbolt from the top of a mountain. "Sign it," she commanded, ripping the sheet from his machine and pushing it into his hands.

A shudder convulsed him as he read what she had written. He put his hand to his heart exactly like a gunfighter who, for once, has been slow on the draw. Beneath his cruel mustache his gentle mouth sagged in what was probably a smile of submission.

He read aloud, " 'Your offer of compromise, cravenly communicated through my wife and daughter, shows you completely ignorant of those principles for which....' Fidelity, if we send this to him now, on top of the other, they won't even let me finish teaching this semester. They'll run us out of town."

Her eye was like the point of a cutlass. "Then get out the camping equipment. We'll sleep on the road."

"The road to where?"

"How do I know? It's a big country. Oh, it's so much bigger than *they* think. That's what you taught us and now you're stuck with it, Papa."

"It may be a big country. But I'm a teacher, and where will I teach?"

"You don't need a classroom to be a teacher," she said. He was about to protest the shakiness of such a slogan when he realized she was quoting what he had once said. With a mixture of glee and terror he admitted she could probably go on driving him with his own quotes from here to the end of their days. Nevertheless, her softening tone encouraged him to grasp one more time for a lifeline of common sense.

"Fidelity, my love, we've got to think of the children, the sheer number of them."

She rose then, seeming to tower up and up on the stilts of her fury. "Sure we've got many children. And I'm going to have more and more and more. As soon as I can. Oh, you poor, stupid, *great* man. You brought us out to wander in the desert and you're going to take us through. Don't you understand that *yet*?"

"Not exactly," he said. He hitched at his belt. "Not perfectly." He reached for the pen. "Not yet," he said as he signed, "but I suppose I will."

Then came his last hesitation before he let her seal the letter which would send them wandering again. "Fidelity, we'll have to really figure carefully where we can go now."

"We'll find the right place by going there."

He bowed his head a minute, then grinned as if he understood her splendid nonsense better than music. As a husband should, he led the way as they went downstairs to tell the children. To tell the world where it got off.

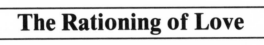

The Rationing of Love

For more than twenty years I was sure my father made too much of the coffee episode. Really, I told him whenever he mentioned the matter, it was nothing, nothing, nothing. I wished he would put it out of his mind. I hadn't taken it seriously to begin with and would long ago have forgotten it if he had.

"But it was only one darn little cup of coffee and you were going *over there*," he always insisted, blaming himself. "I told myself so many times, why, it was only a nickel's worth, but there was all that wartime rationing, you know."

Of course I knew. Had I ever, even for the blink of an eye, refused to accept his first explanation?

The day I went to be drafted in 1942 he refused me a second cup of coffee with my breakfast. He was working as a counterman at the

Bolton & Hay Restaurant in Des Moines, having come up from Gath to attend the summer session at Drake University. He was after the master's degree required for his job as superintendent of the consolidated school in Gath.

I had not seen him since my wedding day. For more than a year I had been serious—giving up my college notions of being a painter so I could support a wife by selling farm implements in her hometown of Waterloo. I mean my first wife, and how odd it seems to think of her as "first wife" in the context of these memories, how odd not to think simply of her name. Ora McGilvery. "Ora means gold," my father told me solemnly at the wedding, implying that I should treat her accordingly.

I had come down alone by bus from Waterloo the evening before I was to be inducted at Camp Dodge. I'd stayed the night in the old Victoria Hotel, a rearing and raffish building whose corridors held some scent of illicit arrivals and departures, some stirring premonition of the worldwide turbulence into which I was being drawn. In my little room I had wakened intermittently at three and four in the morning to hear prowling footsteps outside my door, and when I woke I wondered if my wife was crying in the newness of our first separation. Before daybreak I had made myself think that she was all right, and from that it seemed to follow that everything about to happen to me was going to be all right.

So I felt really good as I walked down from the hotel to meet my father at the Bolton & Hay Restaurant. The hot morning seemed as snappy as the ruffle of drums. The capitol dome gleamed in the radiance of my self-confidence, and the shafts of the Civil War monuments there across the river on the capitol grounds held up their testimony to the bravery of us Midwestern heroes.

A cinder-skinned news butcher was shouting, "Tommies can't stop Rommel!" Maybe the Tommies couldn't, but I was on my way that morning, in the nick of time. Look out, Hitler, here comes Ioway! I guess I really felt a little impatient that I had to stop to see my father at all before I took a bus out to Camp Dodge.

Fortunately my father was ready to share my mood. He wasn't taking the fall of Tobruk very hard. Most of the news he had to tell me was about my mother, brothers, and sister, and the folks in Gath. He wasn't bothered that I'd never "got back to painting" since I left college. He was glad Ora could stay with her parents while I was away. But mostly he was eager to tell me about himself.

There was a countryman's twinkle in his eyes and a conspiratorial lowering of his voice as he told how he had euchred his fellow waiters into letting him have the earliest shift at the lunch counter. "You take a lot of these city people aren't used to getting up till maybe six or seven in the morning. So I told them I'd just as soon come down and open the place up and get the coffee urns going and bring in the bakery stuff and milk. And, shoot, there's hardly anything doing here until after seven. So I have time to read the papers and go over my lessons...."

For his job he wore a white dickey and jacket and a limp little bow tie, innocent as the rags that children wrap around their puppies. He was still deeply tanned from working in his garden at home before the summer-school session had started.

He said, "You take these other fellows who don't come on duty before seven-thirty, why they miss the best part of the day. By the time they have their four hours in, why, I'm back up on the campus and I've had a shower at the field house and a swim if I want to, and I'm out under a shade tree with my books." Four hours of work each day earned him his meals and a dollar in cash that went to help pay his room rent.

While he was watching me eat eggs, bacon, and toast and drink my coffee, he said, "Now you just keep your money in your pocket, son. You may not get civilian food like this for a while, and it's my treat."

Of course I made no argument about that, and since I didn't want any sentimentality to edge in, I kept us talking about his summer. "You've got a pretty soft deal, Dad."

I hadn't meant at all to criticize, but my remark shifted him ever so slightly onto the defensive. "Your mother thinks I just come up to the University to loaf." Well, yes, it was true that my mother kept enforcing a family attitude that he was always too soft to take advantage of his opportunities. "Why," he said, "I'm taking nine hours credit this summer, and with what I've accumulated at Ames and Cedar Falls these last few years I'll get my degree...."

"This summer?"

He didn't even bother to shake his head. "...with a little more extension work and making up my education credits, in nineteen forty-five. I'll bet the war will last at least that long, and the school board won't be likely to push me too hard for my degree as long as all those fellows are in the service and teachers hard to find."

"It won't take us till forty-five, Dad," I said, with the first queasy tremor of doubt I'd felt all morning.

"Who knows? You know, Buddy, your mother even said it didn't seem very dignified for a man my age to be working a board job like you boys did when you went to college. But shoot, I don't know what dignified is if it isn't being willing to do what has to be done."

I was glad then and later that he had said this to me before I left. For too many years while I was a kid at home I'd sided with the other children and my mother in a disrespectful tolerance of his weakness in the face of the school boards who sent us packing every three or four years from town to town, of his kid-glove treatment of the schoolmate bullies who used to knock my brothers and me around for no better reason than that we were the "superintendent's kids." We had blamed him—not too harshly, but persistently—when he let himself be cheated by the small-town garagemen and merchants who took advantage of him because he was a public employee dependent on their good will. We were used to resenting him—a little—because he didn't "stand up to people" and show off his dignity.

I liked him awfully much for telling me his side of all that old misery, but I only said, "I've got to run, Dad. Can I have another cup of coffee before I go to camp?" In a sort of embarrassment I waved my empty cup at him. It's funny how I remember that cup—a big awkward piece of restaurant crockery with two thin green bands painted around it.

He hesitated a minute, thinking. "Well, I'd like to son...." He tried to grin when he shook his head and his grin began to hurt us both.

"I don't really want any," I said quickly.

"You know we're trying to do our bit with coffee rationing."

"I *know*."

"It's only that the boss says...."

"It was an awfully good breakfast, Dad."

"Now, you keep that money in your pocket. No sir, I'm paying for this. Do you need anything? You're going?" He was out from behind the counter quicker than I ever saw him move. As he walked to the door he put his arm over my shoulder, and as we stepped into the explosive sunlight of the street he kissed me quickly on the forehead. He hadn't kissed me since I was five.

He had unbuckled his wristwatch and was trying to fasten the old, sweated band around my arm. "Noticed you weren't wearing one," he said. I let him fasten it, looked at the time, said I'd have to run now to catch the right bus to Camp Dodge.

"Come on back," he said. "Please, come on now, you've got time for one more cup of coffee with me."

But I said I hadn't and that I really, really had drunk all the coffee I needed for a while.

II

In a bad war, in my own worst phases of it, I lucked out with a consistency just short of miraculous. I mean, the miracles were there to be remembered when I had the heart to poke under the garbage for them.

For one thing, on a rain-drenched island as far from combat as it was from any place fit for human habitation, I started painting again while I was convalescing from a rare Asiatic type of diphtheria. It wasn't the throat kind of diphtheria. It spread big colonies of ulcers all over my skin and poisoned me internally so that I was weeks in getting my strength back after the sores cleared up.

Two cultivated ladies named Fitch and Helspur ran the Red Cross hut at the hospital. When they found out I'd had "art training" they not only rummaged out a fine set of oil paints and canvas, they even wanted me to start classes for the other patients. I was too tired for that. Mostly I sat on the back steps of the New Zealand hut they occupied and painted a banana tree on which the bananas were ripening as my abused cell structure mended.

"You're a regular Van Gogh with those yellows," Miss Fitch told me. It was her profession to be flattering.

I put the lovely, creamy brushful of yellow paint back down on the palette, lit a cigarette, and grinned at her through the rising goblin shapes of smoke. I had learned how important it was in my condition and at the juncture of the war in the Pacific to take things easy and slow when you could. She sat down with me and compared the painted yellows with the real bananas.

I said, "You know the first time I ever saw a banana tree? Understand, I always lived in small towns, but my father was a teacher, and he was always going to some college to summer school...."

I'd set her off now. Her father and her uncle and her two great uncles had all been teachers. At Amherst, Smith, and Duke. She herself had been working on her doctorate at Columbia before she joined the Red Cross. She understood *exactly* what it meant to come from "a family of educators."

While she was running on enthusiastically I shook my head slow and steady. "No, no, no. It wasn't like that for us. My father only went into teaching to raise enough money to buy a farm. He kept on because the family kept growing, that's all. He started out a long time ago with not much more than an eighth-grade education. It took him almost twenty years of summer schools to get his B.A. *Anyhow*, depending on which college we lived nearest, he used to go off to

Cedar Falls, or Ames, or Drake. From the time I was very small I remember his bringing the whole family over to see where he was going to college. Next to the stuffed zebras and whale skeletons in the natural history collections, what I remember best is the greenhouse at the college in Cedar Falls where they had a banana tree just like that one.''

''Wonderful!'' Miss Fitch said. I could tell she was picturing my father as some grave and stately academician teaching us kids the Latin names of the rare flora—while what my father had said was, ''Imagine that! Bananas growing right here in Iowa! Look at 'em growing upside down!''

Because she was such an enthusiastic listener, I told Miss Fitch, ''Once when he was in summer school at Ames he took me to see the great, wonderful indoor swimming pool they had there. Imagine that! But it *was* great and wonderful to me. I'd never seen anything like it. The reverberations of the boards in there when the guys dived, the color of the water...the color of that chlorinated water was just like the water up around Ulithi, and the mortar shells around us when we were wading in...I tell you I'd heard them before when Dad took me to that swimming pool and the diving boards rumbled.''

I picked up my brush again from the palette and my hand was trembling. I wasn't any Van Gogh and I didn't any longer expect to be, but the painting—and the associations between one banana tree here and another back there—were making a bridge I needed to live by.

''It makes all the difference if you come from a family of educators,'' Miss Fitch said, far away in her dream of an Amherst girlhood. It didn't matter that I could never explain to her the petty quarrels in my ''family of educators''—about how much of our homemade furniture we'd take with us when we moved from one rinky-dink town to another; whether they should sell my mother's piano after she forgot how to play it; whether the school board hadn't promised to find Dad a lot to keep our cow in when they hired him.

''I'm sure you came by your interest in art from *them*,'' Miss Fitch said.

''Sure. My mother was a frustrated artiste of the piano,'' I said lightly. ''Naturally, at least one kid had to carry on the yokel dream of busting out of the small town. What does it matter? All that's in the bag now, anyway. Next week or the week after—whenever they cut my orders and there's a ship going that way—I'll go up to Okinawa to join my outfit.''

Now knowing how much she'd helped with a miracle, Miss Fitch promised that when I left she and Miss Helspur would pack my new canvases and see that they got home to my wife.

I lucked out, too, when I fell off a troopship in Buckner Bay at Okinawa. The war was over then and we were loading to go home. We were loading from a small boat onto the S.S. Sherman. Tom Hartman was ahead of me on the ladder. I suppose our weird, larking gratitude for surviving the war had become a kind of hysteria. So we were horsing around and it was my own foolish fault that I lunged for the guard rope, missed it, and pitched into the bay.

It happened, too, that I was wearing a field pack full of souvenirs as I fell. That made a bad outfit for swimming. So when I went down headfirst past the small boat, I thought the surprised faces of the boatmen might be the last ones I would ever see.

I went deep before I could get the pack off my shoulders. First I couldn't understand that I had to let it go. Then, as the green of the water got darker around me, the pack clung as if it owned me—that bag full of Okinawa pottery, Japanese pistols, a stained battle flag, and a wooden Buddha I'd looted from a house split open by shellfire. It held onto me like someone drowning who was afraid to let me live if I couldn't take him back up with me.

I don't remember shaking loose from it. All at once I was rising fast and the weight was gone. The strangling water fell away from my face. I saw the boatmen's hands reaching down for mine.

So far so good, but in the same glance I saw my father's wristwatch streaming bright droplets. My first coherent thought as the Navy men were hauling me into their boat was: I finally ruined it for him.

Then all the superstitions I'd been nourishing for three years of war began to concentrate on that ruined watch. I remember how wildly I talked about it to Tom Hartman that night as the ship wallowed east toward home. "I should have got it back to him in the condition he gave it to me."

"Does your father make a lot out of little gestures like that?" he wanted to know.

"I do, whether he does nor not." Then I remembered and laughed. "He's as bad as I am. He'll want to buy me a cup of coffee the minute he sees me." I told Tom what had happened the day I was inducted.

He said, "Well, you better let him buy it for you."

All at once I went morose. I suppose the aftereffects of nearly drowning were coming up on me the way a pain in the jaw comes when the Novocaine wears off. "No, that's silly," I said. "Nothing's going to put things back the way they were before we left. It's too late for some of the things we missed. Are you scared about going home?"

I wish he had said he wasn't. All too easily he knew what I was talking about. "Everybody our age, everybody who's been over as long as we have is a little bit scared. You hear it from everybody," he said. After a while he said, "That's silly. What's to be scared of? Lights, music, girls...?"

We didn't say it, but we were afraid of having permanently lost the track of our lives. Mine—up to the day I'd been drafted—had been nothing but fooling around, as if I'd just been killing time until the war came and a use was found for me. "I found a job just so I could get married," I said. "I wasn't even good at it, or at anything else. So what now?"

"So you might as well have drowned this afternoon." I didn't blame him at all for saying it. He was a man with worries of his own.

I had the mental, moral shakes that night, trying to add up the score of my life in the world as I'd seen it—and coming out with a big round goose egg as of that hour. Coming out with a kind of sad contempt for what I'd grown up trusting. I remembered one time when my father gave the commencement address at Chesterfield for a graduating class of twelve. I had to go to all his public speeches when I was little. Usually I hadn't listened. This time, though, I'd listened because he was talking about Grandpa, whom I'd loved more than anybody. Grandpa, he said, had got in some land dispute with a neighbor. There had been talk among the farmers about how the quarrel could come to a knifing. This neighbor—who must have been a wild man in a generally peaceable community—actually got to carrying a pig sticker with him and showing it at the country store and saying what he meant to do with it.

One day he came by on the road in a spring wagon while my father and Grandpa were raking hay. My father told how Grandpa climbed the fence, went to the middle of the road, and stopped this wild guy, then walked up to him and put out his hand to shake.

That's all there was to the story, and there was my dad up in front of that squirming audience that couldn't care less, him with his bow tie and his soft little grin, holding out his hand to show how it was done. That was his idea of how all problems, domestic and foreign, could probably be handled.

Ah, but behind our ship as I recalled this were the dead cities of Okinawa and Japan. By now the first snow had fallen on the flat cinders of Hiroshima, Nagoya, and the rest. There was Naha blasted into rubble and Shuri Castle where the artillery had blown away everything but the foundations of the ancient walls. With things like that right behind us, who could take seriously a little quarrel so easily mended on a dirt road in southern Iowa?

There was no connection anymore. Before I slept that night I took my father's watch topside and threw it into the froth of our wake. I could be as superstitious as any man in the Army—and believe that watch was the charm that had seen me through. The same superstitions, and a lot more besides, told me it was useless from here on out.

III

The real miracle of those years was what had happened to Ora. She had grown up while I was away. Without any such melodramatic gesture as tossing a watch into the ocean, she had loosened the ties with her parents. She made it instantly clear to me that I wasn't going back to a futureless job in Waterloo. She had moved to Chicago before I shipped up to Okinawa, and the first thing that faced me when I walked into her apartment on Dearborn Street were some of the banana-tree paintings Miss Fitch and Miss Helspur had sent home. She had also hung up some older things I had done in college.

There was only a sundown light in the room when we came in from the taxi, a poor light that made the paintings look better than they were. The yellow bananas glowed like candle flames against a green background more mysterious than the jungle around the Red Cross hut on the island I'd never see again.

"They're not exactly works of genius," I said when I had switched on the apartment lights.

Ora shook her dark head stubbornly. "All right. Not yet. They're going to be."

I said, "Sure. Turn out the lights again. That improves them."

"We're going to New York," she said. "You're going to study at the Art Students League. Of course you are. You've got the GI bill and you've got me. I'm an economic asset. I've got a job there already. I mean I'm almost sure I have. We might, we just might even have a place to live, though that's tougher in New York than here, even."

"A decent job?" I asked.

She made a face at me, a good-natured grimace, but she was disappointed by my caution. "Oh, don't talk like your father or my father or we'll never get anywhere. If New York won't have us, we'll keep going. We'll go on to Paris. Why not?"

"Now you're talking worse than my mother," I said. "There's no use in that."

"I'm not talking like anybody. I'm talking about *us*."

Let it be understood that our conversation was taking place almost the instant I had returned from twenty-eight months overseas. We had not even kissed yet since we came into the apartment, though we had kissed hard and well when she met me at the station and in the taxi that brought us to the North Side. All the anxiety and hope of my return had avalanched into this moment of decision.

And though we had much more to figure out before we left, I knew from then on that we would go. She had challenged me to put up or shut up about all I knew had fallen short in my parents' lives. I said, "O.K."

Then Ora was kneeling beside me in the wide easy chair, kissing me and rubbing her tears all over my face. "You're going to have your chance. You'll be a great painter," she said. Beyond the fringe of her hair I saw the charcoal velvet silhouette of buildings beyond our little window, a sky the color of a wonderful slice of melon. I had a painter's eye, all right. But it took Ora to show me that even Chicago was not a big enough town to hold us.

Paris was our city. New York didn't seem to have room for us that year. We went past it with a lordly air and borrowed boat fare. Paris was home for several years, and I keep thinking we should have been happy there, since we both loved it so much. But we weren't. Our years there provided "the foundation of my career," as it says in the brochure printed just last year by the gallery in Chicago that handles my painting, now that I've come back to work and teach in the Midwest. There never was a young couple in Paris who got more excitement and pleasure in discovering the fine parks, the old splendors of cathedrals and chateaux, places to eat and buy things, the displays of weather over the Seine, and the way the trees would darken secretly in the Luxembourg Gardens after the steel gates were closed for the night across the street from our apartment.

Too rich for our blood? There was a fault somewhere.

Ora worked first for an American oil company and later for the American Embassy. In the first years I walked alongside the Luxembourg Gardens every morning on my way to the Grande Chaumiere where I was painting with Leger. Paris was very poor in those years just after the war, and we weren't. We had a sports car pretty soon for summer trips into the Loire valley and the Dordogne. When Ora went to the embassy we had PX privileges, American goodies for ourselves and for the black market. Happy or not, we lived the big life, and we stayed long enough to see Paris change again into the prospering capital of the world. Among the Fulbright students and other new waves of young Americans we were accepted as old settlers.

I was painting pretty well. I was making contacts with people who could do me some good.

Letters from my parents in those years came like drafts from a window one has forgotten to close before lying down for a warm nap. My mother's indicated she thought we were living an idealist missionary life—presumably weaning the French away from their bad habits of drinking wine, making love indiscriminately, and abusing their colonial peoples. She hoped we would not have children until we got back to the shelter of American sanitation.

My father, who only wrote short notes at Christmas or for our birthdays, seemed to make no distinction between my being "over there" among the Bohemians and my having been "over there" with the Army. I used to read his letters in my favorite cafe on the square at St. Sulpice and parody them for my friends. I would remember them with a kind of terrible nostalgia while I was getting stewed in the *caves* around St. Germain—or at the Select, in the winter of Eleanor. One night when the police picked me up for riotous behavior in Montparnasse I went into a yelling fit in the back of the *salade panier*, the police van. The next day I could remember only that I had been trying to tell my father I was a long time out of the Army and the damned South Pacific and nobody was giving me orders anymore.

If there ever was a chance to clear up such truths for him, I had it when I came back to Iowa in 1954 to tell my parents why Ora divorced me. They hadn't known her well, but they cared about her and knew that I had, too.

So my efforts to be scrupulous in my explanations only confused them further. They wouldn't believe me. They wouldn't comprehend that it had been all my fault instead of the fault of the corrupt French environment. They couldn't quite see why, just because I took some initial interest in the paintings of a Fulbright student named Eleanor Marshall, I should have run off to Africa with her. Or why, when the intoxications of novelty wore off with the drugs we got from the Algerians, Eleanor and I had begun a hesitant, slow circling back toward Paris. I could recall the nastiness and despair of those weeks in Alexandria and the days in Naples, but I just lacked the language to tell the old folks our great sin excursion collapsed because we had used up the money I stole from Ora and saved from black-marketing PX goods.

I heard my own voice tell them these things. I doubt if they heard much. They were living now in another small Iowa town where again my father was teaching. The house to which I had come was excruciatingly like the other houses I remembered living in while I was growing up. The same dark, small living room, the same softwood floors varnished dark, the same high school graduation pictures of my brothers, sister, and me on the piano that had been moved so often and played so little.

It was early summer and the kitchen windows were open as we sat at supper. A light rain was falling on the potted flowers my mother had set on a shelf outside the windows to get some fresh air. My mother said, "I suppose that Eleanor will be coming back soon to join you."

I shook my head carefully, as if I might spatter filth over her clean kitchen if I shook too hard. "She's not going to join me, Mama. She came to New York before I did. I'm not going to see her, didn't I make that clear?"

It was lucky my fingernails were chewed short or I might have drawn blood from the clenching of my hands. The last thing I'd wanted from this visit was the kind of dull sympathy I was getting. Maybe in some dream I had expected I was going to be punished here, like the time I was punished for shooting at the Alleman girl with my air rifle when we lived in Chesterfield.

"I don't understand much about divorces," my mother said, still resisting, still sure things could be arranged for the best, "but it seems to me there's no reason you and she can't be married if you wanted to as bad as all that."

I remembered Eleanor and me lying side by side on a bed in a bad hotel in Rome. It was raining outside that room, too, but it was very cold there so the chill came right through the walls. We'd lain fully dressed with nothing to say to each other, merely passing a rare cigarette back and forth, waiting for the day to be over. The moisture of our lips on the cigarette paper was the only intimacy between us by then.

"At least we'll be spared marriage, whatever other payment we still have to make."

I'm not sure my mother caught the full savagery of what I'd said. My father did. He'd never been stretched past the point of endurance by the untouchable loveliness of my Paris, never seen with a painter's hopeless eye the high white clouds over Oran in the inexpressible Mediterranean light. How could he imagine Eleanor's strange mouth ready to be kissed? He only thought my paintings were "all right if there's people want to buy such things." But he knew what counted.

While I had been talking to my mother he had risen from the supper table. He stood at the window and his hands reached outside, fumbling with or caressing the wet geranium leaves.

After a while he said, "Darn it, I've thought so many times, why didn't I give you that second cup of coffee when you were going away?"

As if that one thing alone might have saved me from all my delinquencies! As if without this one default of courage he might have kept me true!

IV

My mother nearly died last fall. She dwindled and grew dull through the spring and summer. Each time I drove over from Illinois with my wife and three young children she seemed progressively less interested in finding toys from the attic for the little ones, even less sure of their names. Getting old, we said.

Then she fell down the basement stairs while she was bringing in flower bulbs from the garden about to freeze. She may have hit her head in the fall. She was very confused and dazed afterward. But when she was taken to the hospital in Des Moines the main source of her trouble was diagnosed as a tumor of the spleen, which had been seriously affecting her blood-sugar level. This had been going on long enough to suggest there might have been brain damage before her tumble.

Occasionally, when we visited her in the hospital, she would seem like her old self. These were times when she had been given medicine to counter the insulin surplus and had taken a lot of extra sugar in her orange juice. When my father, brothers, and sister hovered around her bed she could still beam and chatter and press our hands and thank us for "coming all that way" to be with her at such a time. "All that way...." Perhaps she still thought I was living in Paris. At any rate, her quaint manner of putting it made me remember all my travels as if they were a single journey toward this time of anguish.

With extraordinary effort she could remember each of her grandchildren. When I prompted her, she asked about my children individually and by name. Were they anxious for snow? Did they like kindergarten and school?

But she was frightened, too. Sometimes, even at her most lucid moments and even when all of us were with her, she would ignore her children and speak only to my father. She questioned him about insurance, about the burial plot they had arranged for in the yard of the church where they were married, and about whether someone was taking care of her plants while she was away.

We saw that she always scared him with such talk. "You're not going to die, Mother," he told her over and over again—while the rest of us resolutely avoided any mention of death in her presence.

Often we found her out of her head—when the level of her blood sugar was not being artificially maintained—and she raved her distrust of the doctors who came several times a day to "bother her" and "wasted so much time" in getting it over with.

Her operation, when it took place, was mercifully briefer and luckier than we had been led to expect by the doctors. Her tumor was benign. Very little exploratory surgery was needed to locate it, though it had not showed in the x-rays.

Nonetheless, some ultimate transformation had been wrought on her in those hours when she was under anaesthetic. I was alone with her in the recovery room—we were permitted to go in to her only one at a time—when the fog of ether was leaving her. She was discovering that her right arm was bound to a board to keep the intravenous tube in place, and she fought the bondage piteously, trying to tear the tube out of the vein. Another tube was taped over her forehead and into her right nostril. I restrained her as gently as I could. She hated me for siding with all her other persecutors.

"They have no right to an old lady," she said. "Cut her all open. Bring her in here and cut her body." There was a horrifying strength in the free hand that wrestled against mine to get at the IV tube. Then she became aware of the other tube in her nose. "What's that for, too?" she said, and clawed for it.

I had to call a nurse, and we tied both hands down to make her leave the tubes alone.

She hadn't the strength to raise her head, of course. The hatred in her eyes was like the blow of a fist. She glared at me as if I were her murderer. "You have no right," she said.

"It won't be long now, Mama," I said. "I know you're very uncomfortable right now. They'll give you something for the pain and to make you sleep."

"Oh, the pain," she said. "Untie me. Let me loose."

"No. I won't."

"*Let me loose!*" Her voice was like a man's, compelling and brutal. Perhaps if the nurses had not been working nearby I might have done what she demanded.

"I can't let you loose," I said. "You'll be all right. You'll sleep. You'll rest. You'll sleep."

She turned her head to the side. Her crepey cheek was almost as crimson as blood from the great effort she was making. The tears on her cheek were tears of anger. "Why didn't they get it over with?"

"It's not going to be over," I said. "Don't you understand? You didn't have cancer. You'll be all right. It will take a while to get your strength back, but you're going to be fine."

"Why?"

I'm not certain she meant anything by this syllable. Surely I shouldn't have tried to answer then. But I said, "Why, because we need you. We all need you. My children, too. They've been wanting to come and see Grandma and go up into the attic with her again. Play the piano with her...."

Now she knew exactly what she had to say. It was as if she had always been trying to clarify it. She said it now with a last, hoarded emphasis of deliberation. "No one has any right to bring children into the world." She meant me. She meant my sons. Our wickedness and our suffering had been from her, and she repented us. "Where's Ora? Where's your wife?" she asked with awful scorn. "Ora had no children. What have you done with her?"

I said nothing.

She smiled a little, a smile of terrible cruelty. "We have no right," she said tiredly. Then—perhaps she was sinking back into the vision or dream that had deviled her while she was on the operating table.

"The children are burning everywhere," she said vaguely.

It was less than an hour after that when my father and I walked down the hill from the hospital in the November sun. I saw that my shadow was longer than his on the concrete slope ahead of us, but his step was jauntier than mine. As if he didn't know yet—as if he was never going to find out—the truth my mother had just told me.

"The doctor said it was no bigger than a fingertip," he said of the tumor that had been removed from her. "Boy, the doctor said it was certainly good luck they found it so quick when the x-ray couldn't find it."

"We've been very lucky."

"Well, we sure have." He took a long trembling breath. It sounded like my youngest boy when he has been crying hard and is trying to reestablish a normal rhythm of breathing. "And you know, lucky with the Blue Cross and all. Just couldn't have been luckier."

He had a right to his relief, but I was suspicious of its excess and warned him, "She's not going to be the same, Dad."

"Why," he said, "why, I know that. Why, *of course not.* We're getting older, and all."

"She's in her seventies. It isn't going to be easy for her to make a comeback."

"*Of course* it won't. And I don't know what's the best thing to plan. The doctor said that, well, maybe the best thing for me to count on is to put her in a nursing home awhile because her convalescence might be months, and he thought I wouldn't be much of a hand for taking care of her."

It might well be more than a matter of months. The doctors to whom I had spoken avoided the word *convalescence.* She was too old. There was no return from the descent she had begun. "We ought to consider a nursing home," I said cautiously.

"Why, why, I told him *no!* Why I'd crawl on my hands and knees to take care of her before I'd let them take her away."

He tossed that off as a matter of fact. So jauntily. I doubted if he had even weighed the realities of what might be still to come. He just knew what he had to do—and I envied him for that as I never expected to envy another human being. All his life with us we had thought him too soft, gentle but a little foolish—and he had nursed his courage in the shade of soft foolishness until the time to use it well had come. I knew that, and the wonderful thing is that I think he knew it too.

"Well," I said, "well. We better turn and go back to the hospital."

"Just down that next block. All right?"

I had supposed we were merely getting a breath of fresh air before we rejoined the rest of the family in the vigil at the hospital.

No. He had known exactly where he was leading me. In the next block was the Bolton & Hay Restaurant where I'd said goodbye to him when I went in the Army. Suddenly there we were, in front of it.

"You know, son," he said with his old easy, floppy smile, "you know there's something that's bothered me...."

Of course I knew what was coming, and I wanted no part of it. He had no trick to play except a sentimental one, and that was not nearly enough. The things we had done wrong with our lives were signed, sealed and irretrievable. Ora was gone; I had my new wife and children. My mother was going to live, but her faith in life had not lasted quite as long as her outraged body. I had paid more than a man should choose to pay for my small share of success. My mother had not touched her piano for thirty years. We had been lucky to come this far with a divided verdict.

We had been lucky. My father said so and I believed him. But I saw now that the reckless old fool wanted still to gamble for more. I

114

caught my breath as if watching a clownish acrobat preparing to challenge the trim, athletic professionals on the high wire. He was going to insist you *could* go back, in spite of time, and make the past all right.

"Now," he said, rather formally. "I could just as well have given you that cup of coffee you asked for that morning. Just as well as not."

His trick depended on just one thing—on my willingness to believe in it, at the price of all I'd paid so much to learn. I guessed I could if I wanted to. Nothing was stopping me.

I said, "Well, since we're here, why don't you get it for me now?" The worst had been ahead of us. Now it was behind us. Both of us could claim that much victory.

He said that to give me the coffee I had asked for was just exactly what he intended to do.

Like a boy, I followed him into the restaurant.

Marriage

Dad's younger brother developed a habit that led to his being called "Marrying Joe." In his lifetime Joe married six or seven women and involved himself with an uncounted bevy of others. But Joe had been to World War I where righteousness was notoriously shredded and scattered, and he came back to Iowa to live in Des Moines where temptation lay on every hand. Joe also became a lush and perhaps took on or shed off his women in some stage of inebriation. All this is to say that in fact and spirit he went farther from the farm in southern Iowa than Dad could ever go.

Dad was a teacher in small town schools for all his working life, therefore the latitude for scandalous behavior was slight. Now and then—rarely—rumors would spread about him and one or another of the high school girls who worked for him in his office, but I am convinced that the rumors came from idle mischief and had no basis in fact. And if the communities where he taught held a tight rein on him, so did my mother. She was simply fiercer and more determined on all counts than he. It would hardly have been worth the while of a peace-loving man to try any deceptions.

Knowing his circumspect behavior for so long, then, my brothers, sister, and I were more than slightly shocked when he began an almost reckless campaign of courtship very soon after our mother's death. A squirming, sighing, clucking, uneasy disapproval shook the family like a neural disturbance—something we could hardly confess soberly to ourselves, something we usually spoke about with faked amusement.

"You know, he even proposed to Esther Boyle," my sister reported. "Esther Boyle naturally told everyone, and she thought it was pretty silly." I clucked my regret at the proposal and the gossip. Esther Boyle had been a neighbor and casual friend of Mom's. They traded produce from their gardens and informed each other of the passage of shady characters. But Esther was famously decrepit and deeply established in her widowhood. If my father had targeted her he must be so desperate there was no guessing how wildly he might range in his quest.

Then again he might be shooting blanks in a playful spree, intending nothing beyond sport in a game he had so little chance to play. Soon he might relapse into his schoolteacher character and cool down. With, I suppose, some intent of monitoring his behavior, my brother and his wife took him home with them to the county seat where they lived. This arrangement was supposed to give him a home environment that would keep him from wobbling onto the path where his younger brother Joe had strayed. (None of the family had ever seen much of Joe; no one knew the details of his life and liaisons; but as a somewhat comic warning example he was very much a functioning part of the family. He had set a benchmark for measuring marital values.)

The tactic seemed to have the intended effect on Dad. Moving to a larger town gave him more to occupy his time. He spent many docile afternoons on the benches of the city park. He got acquainted with neighborhood children and cheerfully did shopping errands for my sister-in-law. He responded to notices of senior citizens' gatherings and dressed up with his best bow tie and straw hat to attend them. Sometimes he would take the bus downtown and hang around the courthouse steps or visit the hospital to strike up conversations with other elderly people. But by piecing together his reports of these excursions my brother and his wife sniffed out his real intent. Dad was sizing up the older women, measuring them all for suitability and, as far as we knew, scattering proposals up and down the hospital corridors, in the anterooms of civic buildings and in the shady nooks of the park. Or maybe just trying to overcome his shyness so he could make one credible proposal to a woman he could imagine living with.

"We're prepared," my sister-in-law wrote, "to have him come home from an afternoon walk with a lady in tow and just announce to us we have to lay another place for supper because he's just married her. Excuse me. We are NOT prepared for that. We're just real glad for him to stay with us for a little while. But in the long run, he better be thinking of a good, clean old people's home, because you know as well as I that he's not going to find anyone to take care of him and make a home for him the way your mother did when she was well. And where would they live anyway, really?"

Then for a little while Dad seemed to have struck pay dirt. Or he drew on resources none of us knew he had. From out of his college past there reappeared a woman named Edna Halvorsen, said to be wealthy after the death of a husband in real estate, said to be lively, said to be inclined toward matrimony again even in her seventieth year. I heard about her directly from my father when we met by arrangement in the Kansas airport. He was flying to Arkansas to visit the lady. I was going further west.

"Here," he said with a timid smile. He pulled some glossy photos from his jacket pocket and offered them to me. It almost made my knees buckle that his showing the photos should be so tentative and anxious, as if I might have said, "She won't do." As if he would have made his crestfallen way back home if my expression had registered any disapproval.

"She's a very handsome woman," I said. "Nice eyes."

"She's got a very accomplished family. All grown up, of course. Fine grandchildren. She plays the piano."

It was not my place to ask where she was going to play that piano in case they actually got married, any more than it was my place to ask anything at all about where and how he had known her in times before my memory. I pretended conversation but essentially I was mute.

"She does a lot of reading. She belongs to the Book of the Month Club. She enjoys Bingo evenings and the religious services at the senior citizen group. I think we will get along fine, don't you?"

"You haven't actually seen her yet?"

"Oh yes, I have. She was in Des Moines visiting with her sister a little while back. This will be my first visit to her home."

It sounded pretty shaky to me. He sounded shaky. In so far as I could muster confidence he was on the right track, I wished him luck.

And to this day I am convinced he almost pulled it off with the Arkansas widow. After his first persuasive advance into Arkansas, the widow flew twice to Iowa to keep the negotiation going. Then, I heard, it was all over. The parties had agreed it could not be. Arkansas was too far away, perhaps. Perhaps they had both reached out eagerly across a stretch of years and circumstances too great for them to overcome. Though I had seen only a few small, unglamorous photos of a woman with a soft mop of white hair and ornate spectacle frames over cheeks bulging like mushrooms, my sympathies doctored her image as I thought of her. In a way, I guess, she became not only the allegory of my father's longing but of a curious desire he had transplanted in me. Did she not, perhaps, resemble Mae West in the rougish twinkle of her eyes? No, of course not Mae West nor anyone so public, but surely some small town vamp of extraordinary plumage. In her life she had preserved some vivacious secret flame my father had been lucky to sniff out. The fact is, it gave me a genuine, oblique, erotic glow to ponder this elder stranger and her preserved treasures of gossamer and fire. Oh, I saw her as if Dad were my seeing-eye dog tugging toward some majestic womanhood I could never behold with my own jaded senses. And in lapses of consciousness, I could hear this seductress tinkling jazz on her piano. So I mourned Dad's loss. He had burned with a slow flame all his life. Now it seemed his one chance to flare intensely was gone.

In this mood of loss I guessed his courting to be a search for compensation for those many years Mom had taken the hide off him with her outspoken frustrations and the shafts of blame for them she buried in his docile back. He had never been quite equal to the harsh demand of living with her while they begot us children and raised us.

Mom was stung with ambition of the kind available to poor people who know they are always going to be poor. She thought our rented houses could be a "little better" if we all pitched in to paper the walls, varnish the softwood floors, and lay a little paint on the peeling exteriors. She thought the family diet would reach a higher standard of nourishment if we kept a cow and chickens and raised large gardens full of vegetables recommended by the agricultural college. She thought the Sunday School could be more enlightened if both she and Dad contributed their time and their "ideas" to the teaching. Naturally he had no appetite for extra teaching beyond what he was paid for and he wasn't aware of any ideas he might have to contribute to seekers after religion. The ideas were the ones she brooded over during a week of housework and were mostly offensive to the local churchfolk. She was a woman to whom ideological principle was much more important than making friends. It can't be said that she ever eased his community standing by a strategy of friendship.

He never criticized her outright for riling preachers and parishioners. I suppose he didn't dare. Having the schoolboard go against him, as it did in each town at about four-year intervals, was bad enough. He didn't need at home the sort of hostility and doctrinal reasoning she was capable of when the truth was clear to her.

"Did they love each other ever?" my sister asked at a family reunion some time after they were both dead. "Did they to begin with, do you suppose?"

Reunions are times for optimistic solidarity, so we airily agreed that they must have. Surely, we said. All marriages have their honeymoons. And the parts of loyal memory that feed on the driest and most infrequent crumbs of solace find a little treasure where they can.

"Dad always remembered driving Old Dan when he courted her," we recalled. And someone produced a very faded snapshot of Dad beside a buggy to which was hitched a sleek horse named Old Dan. Unarguably both Dad and the horse looked happy. They looked ready to go. They were a moment of youth and they were on their way to some hour or place of infallible enchantment where Mom in her young womanhood would welcome them, receive the eagerness offered. Around Old Dan trotting down a soft dirt road in the moonlight of midsummer the imagination can create a large, sweet landscape of love, for one has been there himself, or some place so like it that all the great hopes and fidelities can be reconstructed from it for the sake of the dead. Yes, yes, sure our parents embraced and knew what is to be known of love.

And there are other snapshots—interiors—posed to show them in their young tranquility, where he is reading a book, as a schoolteacher should, and she is placidly, dreamily sewing. They are standing beside a Model T, ready for a Sunday outing with the children tucked on board looking content at the promise of going to the lake.

They were all right, say the treasured snapshots. They suffered the common lot with its share of sabbaths. The fine times are not canceled by the whispers that accompany them and make the other part of memory.

The little we have of truth comes to us diluted and from far away. Certainly there is evidence of things unseen. There are times we must choose it ahead of any other. I never saw Old Dan strut on moonlit, soft roads, but I am persuaded he was a fine horse for anyone to ride behind. I would go now if anyone said: Let's take Old Dan out for a trot this evening. On the other hand, though I got it as hearsay and opinion, my judgment was permanently slanted by what I heard Mom say on so many occasions when where was grief in the house in my childhood: "He's not a bad man like his brother Joe turned out. He doesn't drink or swear or go with bad women. He's just weak." I knew she was not uttering this as accusation. She was uttering her own cry from an entrapment they shared and must endure. I remember especially once when she broke loose with this pronouncement, a time when she had been physically hurt in one of her chores and was sitting with her leg in a tub of hot water to ease some pustular infection that immobilized her. The February night was blowing snow outside our flimsy house, and the chances are Dad had escaped for a while by going down to the school for a basketball game. She could not have intended that the children who sat trying to comfort her should imagine Dad capable of cruel or even unkind things. She was bearing witness to others who knew him, and her complaint came down to this: there was no man there to lift her beyond her present misery and the wretchedness that had settled on her like a habit. But then, setting her jaw so she could smile, straining the cords of her neck, she said with a cry of pride, "Why once when he was young and he was at a church sociable, one of the kerosene lamps burst out in flames, and he went right for it, and he grabbed it and carried it outside before any damage could be done, and it burned his hand badly." She drew no moral from this. There is probably no moral to draw. In a fine moment he had done something heroic. Usually he did not. There is no gain at all in reflecting that is the pattern in most lives.

She settled again on her definition of him as weak when, rather early in their marriage, he began to buy a farm on a mortgage. After he got a feel of what it was like, Dad never really meant to be a teacher. In his unflagging optimism and vulnerability to salesmen, it occurred to him that on a teacher's salary he could own a farm in a better part of the state than he and Mom had come from. I suppose my mother neither encouraged him nor discouraged him from going ahead with the deal.

But when he lost all the money he had paid into the mortgage, her grief about the loss was palpable and permanent. She did not need direct accusation to make the whole family understand a stronger man would somehow have climbed right over the bankers and claimed the land he had promised us all. Her sense of right and wrong had been permanently shaped by the Biblical reading of her girlhood and obviously my father cut a poor figure when measured by Biblical heroes.

Undismayed, when we had moved to another town, Dad bought a ramshackle house for investment and spent a grueling summer painting it and putting it in repair. Again he lost his labor and some money, as a stronger man would not.

When my brother had to postpone starting to college, Mom talked to me very soberly, seeing it as a foreshadowing of my own prospects. "There's no reason for this. A little better planning and we could have made it. When you're grown up you must always try to plan. Your father didn't do this on purpose. He didn't plan well."

Once with an expression of profound sadness on her face, she said— surely more to herself than to me—"I used to think I could help him. I thought I could teach him to get along in practical life."

She seldom nagged him straightforwardly, just as she seldom gave him a day or a week without some observation of his inadequacies to disturb him. One day his shirt wasn't clean. Or he had missed a chance to get a bargain on auto supplies by failing to read the ads. His manners were below standard for a teacher who was supposed to be an example for the young.

To watch them arguing politics was like watching boxers going into a ring. By well established habit they slid into opposite corners and faced off. The lines of argument were usually between "what most people thought" (his position) and her vehement pronouncement of what they shouldn't think if they had any sense of right and wrong.

"A lot of people say Roosevelt has done a lot of people good," he found.

She knew he got this opinion from listening to the no-goods down at the gas station or even from the pool hall. Shaking her frying pan to make the grease sizzle, she said, "Oh I know! What kind of people? Just those who hang around all day waiting for someone to come and give them something for nothing. We work hard for our living, and what do we have? Just look around this room. What do we have?"

"Maybe we should go on relief."

"Oh no. Oh no. People with any gumption can take care of themselves. Will you go to the pump and get us water for the reservoir of the stove? Bring in some firewood too for the dining room heater. We'll make out without any Roosevelt sticking his nose in here."

So it went from town to town and house to house. Scar tissue building and scar tissue peeling like dead skin. Evening out over so many years without any real drama, only the monotone of unsatisfied lives unbelievably persisting.

But remember this, too:

Once they had been quarreling longer and more brutally than usual. The fight this time would have been about one of us children—how we were deprived or mistreated at school where he was supposed to have some authority—as it usually was once their dissatisfaction with each other had heated the coals white hot.

This particular battle was out of scale for them. So Dad locked himself in the bathroom after showing Mom and us children he had a straight razor open in his hand. It is a scene I am unable to reconstruct as having any movement. It is frozen like some aberrant dreams are frozen even while they are present in the night mind. We were simply there motionless in a room where a door had closed. The minds of children, at least, refuse to function on certain details, and we hung in the dim fringes of the action merely hoping, I suppose, that this episode, too, would somehow come out all right. Given the horror we waited for, I am surprised that none of us giggled.

It was Mom's test, fundamentally. It was she who had to face the unthinkable possibility that he might kill himself in there with his razor. The issue was a conflict of wills between a weak man with nothing to put into the contest but his own convulsing, sobbing throat and a tough, proud, embittered woman.

Perhaps it was the time and scene when the marriage took its definition for eternity. So it is my choice to see her as she stood hesitantly before that closed door, her mouth working as she counted the seconds, counted the injustices that had befallen them both in the trials they had known since they rode behind Old Dan in a deceptive springtime. Surely she was tallying Dad's weaknesses, which she claimed were so well known to her. She must have doubted his strength to make good his threat to kill himself. She must have had a strong conviction that the threat was another of his ways of tricking her out of her own position. But there were the children with her, counting breaths and seconds in this terrible rapture. We admitted none of the costs she had borne and would have still to bear. We wanted to see Dad come out of that tiny room on his feet, without blood.

So, with a kind of terrible cruelty to herself, she yielded. Dismantled some secret and precious part of her being, her sense of justice, deep as her life.

I will say we saw her break herself like a stick and offer it—not to a new beginning for the family—there were quarrels after this, perhaps just as bitter—but to the moment when his life depended on her stepping down and back.

"Howard," she called softly through the door. It was the voice of a bride, not contrived, not needing to be contrived and beyond her power to contrive.

She repeated his name and rattled the locked door. There was no audible response but a silence that said he had heard her.

I think he was crying out of our sight, probably looking with a certain incredulity at the blade in his hand, crying in relief that after all he was not obliged to use it to make good his promise.

So, of course, he came out after the little interval his shock, terror, and pride allowed. He was white as a sheet and staggering. He more or less toppled into Mom's arms and she cradled him. "He's all right," she murmured. "You know we can work things out. We'll sit down and talk."

"If only you hadn't...." was all we children heard him say before we fled in a relief so merciful and mighty that it blocked out the worst of what we had seen. It was tagged down as only another in the everlasting series of their conflicts.

But she said, "I was wrong, Howard. You were, too. So that's what we are going to talk about...."

She would have cherished his life, but not given in to him even then. I know it. For in their innocence they had married to be antagonists.

Always sparring, they had their comic turns as well as horrifying ones. At one point they developed a kind of vaudeville routine involving his watch and her clock.

When the family planned a shopping trip to the county seat, it was habitual to set a morning hour for our departure from the house. With flurries and protestation of having much to do to get the whole family ready for the trip, Mom would set her clock for all to see. "I'm setting it half an hour ahead," she claimed, "so I'll be sure to watch it and have everything done in time."

After a few repeats we knew what the outcome would be. At the agreed time Dad would walk into the kitchen dangling his gold watch from the chain. The hour had arrived. But never on her clock. Set ahead, it had probably been reset to fit with her schedule.

"It can't be ten o'clock. My clock doesn't say ten thirty." That was her opener—not intended for rational examination but only as the opening of an argument so devious and intertwined that he simply had to take his watch away and wait until she was finally ready.

Let it be said only that we always went. When a shopping trip or attendance at college was planned, the family made it. The raggedest and meanest kind of cooperation took over somewhere down below all the evidence of discord.

The shrillness of our early lives drove all the children away as soon as we were able to make it on our own. But however we distanced ourselves we were always children of this family. I suppose we were bound as much by shame as by pride, as if we were all accomplices at a crime of many years' duration.

Did they love each other? Could we ever cease loving them in the circumstances of their long bondage? It is not one of those things that is easy to admit.

Even when my mother died it was something of a formality to profess to friends and relatives that, of course, we had loved her dearly, for her sacrifice, for her spirit, and devotion to us all. The right word is the unspeakable one—it is mightier than love and by the same proportion less intelligible.

Dad failed with the Arkansas widow. But did much better in spite of that. Quietly, to the surprise of us all, he married a fine little widow he had met at a senior citizens' party. She helped him with Bingo. He taught her checkers.

Alice had a cozy little house into which Dad moved after a series of old people's homes. She liked to cook for him. She read books to him as his eyesight faded, and they enjoyed the same programs on the radio.

Twice Dad was in the hospital near death in his years of the second marriage. Alice corresponded with us children faithfully during these times and sent birthday and Christmas cards to one and all children and grandchildren.

Living far away by now, I visited them only once in these years. Alice was home alone when I came from the cab to knock at their door.

She had a pleasant smile and a knack for instant mother lines. "Oh your Dad has been so excited you were coming!" she said. She gave me a discreet hug and I liked the smell of her powder and the clean smell of her body.

"Howard's down at the corner shopping for our supper—we hope you like pork chops—that's what I told him to get—and you can just come in and sit if you want until he gets back. Won't you come in?"

Call it bashfulness that I refused and said I would go to meet my father. It was probably something else less creditable. For all her warmth and niceness I found her alien. The warped instincts of my whole childhood simply said: she is not one of us. And I was ashamed but I could not help it.

My father was doddering as he came along the sidewalk with his package from the grocery store. There was nothing firm looking about him but his smile as he recognized me. A year before some teen-aged hoodlum had mugged him and stolen his money on the same path to the store. I was choked with pride at his determination in following the same sidewalk now without caution.

I hugged him and felt the frailty of his shoulder bones above the soft paunch of his slipping torso. But he permitted no occasion then to talk of his health. From the first he wanted to brag about his happy situation with Alice. Before we got back to the house he babbled out a lot. Why, she had been a schoolteacher as he had. They knew a lot of people in common from their years in the profession. "Why she had this house and she said, 'Why we might as well share it together.' It sure is comfortable there and she cooks me about whatever I want. Why we had fried chicken last night. You know, I still like to eat the feet of a fried chicken. But I ate more than that, you bet. My appetite is sure good. And, you know, Alice and I have a regular business arrangement. We're married but the contract says that whatever little property I have will be for you kids, and the house here and whatever she has will be for hers. This was her idea, and I just said, 'Why, what a sensible idea that is.' "

At the meal I shared with them I found no slightest fault with Alice —supposing I had been of a mind to do so. She was a fine and loving wife for Dad, an easy hostess for me. With a certain nice detachment she discussed Dad's illnesses with me, the doctor's concerns and the periods of greatest danger.

"You know, the main thing is that Howard has a fine constitution," she said fondly, laying her hand on his sleeve. "That saw him through, I'm sure." And I am sure that in praising his constitution she was praising his persisting powers as a husband, such as even a handsome elderly woman like she could value.

He said, "Sure do love the way you cook those pork chops so tender." He gnawed one of the chops down close to the bone and wiped his chin with his sleeve.

She chided me gently for not visiting more often and for being a poor correspondent. "Now that we're tied down, it's important to know what you younger people are doing in your careers."

"Not tied down," Dad said happily, reaching himself another

helping of vegetables. "Tell him, Alice, how many church functions and that sort of thing we been to in the last two weeks." And he left the telling to her as he filled up on her cooking.

It was Alice, the next morning, who privately discussed with me the precariousness of his condition. "The doctor says all we can do is wait. But I'm afraid his next trip to the hospital may be his last."

"But he looks well."

She cocked her head and smiled doubtfully.

"You take wonderful care of him."

"I'm proud to do what I can. He's lived a life of service and so many of his students write to say they remember him. He's an old toughie and will keep right on as long as I can keep behind him."

"He's got good years left."

She was not to be swayed into cheerful agreement with me. "Our Maker has a plan for us all," she said gravely.

"Well, he's got you, so his luck is still running strong."

She smiled away the irrelevant praise. From her own appraisal of him she cared for him deeply. Her affection was her wages. She had him for her own at the end of his life. If I read her well, she never wasted time wondering what it might have been like to be married to him from his young days.

As for the last pronouncement he spoke to me face to face, he shuffled with me into the front hall of Alice's house that day when I had to say goodbye. With a faltering voice he said, "I just wanted you kids to know how proud I am of you all. What you made of yourselves. Mom and I couldn't do as much for you as we had wanted, but you did a lot with what was in you. Well, you keep in touch. It's a big day for Alice and me when we get one of your letters from all the places you go."

Faithlessly again I promised to keep him informed of everything. But on that score it was still the same as it had always been since I skipped off to college. I was bound to him always by mute love, too alienated for either candor or fullness. In his lifetime he must have had droves of cronies and acquaintances who answered him more openly than I.

I couldn't even muster the right combination of dread and love to keep track by mail or phone of his failing health. It was he who called me with a querulous complaint one time that he "smelled bad when he took a bath."

"I don't think that means anything," I said.

"Doctors say it doesn't. But I don't know. It's not a smell I ever had before. Alice notices it, but she won't say anything about it. She just helps me keep nice and clean. I don't smell good even after I've bathed.''

I was dazed when I hung up the phone, could not explain to my wife what I had heard. It was as if some code, never used before but utterly transparent, had been invoked to pass news that can never be softened enough.

A few weeks later when I was in Rome he reached me in my hotel room and began just as he would if I were down the block and might drop over to cheer him up. "Son, I've been kind of under the weather again.''

"Have you, Dad?''

"Just not feeling up to myself.''

"I'll bet Alice is taking good care of you.''

"You bet she is! It's sure better being home than being in some darn hospital where they don't care who you are. Alice thinks I won't have to go to the hospital. I tell her if I have to, I will. We'll wait and see.''

"That's what we have to do.''

"Alice and I think about you in that foreign country. We sure do. So she said I'd better make a long distance call.'' He ended with a quaver impossible to misinterpret. He was giving up and meant it to be understood this would be his last communication.

He died of inoperable cancer before I got home to see him again. I can think of no deathbed exchange that would have altered the familiarity which had survived our long separations.

But I did get better acquainted with Alice at his funeral. She did not have to speak to me as a son. There were no debts or remorses running either way to make us shy in speech. We were two people who had both seen him partially. We found we were very well matched in a tempered grief for a man who had lived a long time and had visibly found a share of contentments. It pleased me to hear her strike the same tone with my brothers and sister. She bound us again in family feelings. She merged her fondest memories with ours in a continuing story. We knew through her we were not altogether bereft. I guess it may have been her promptings that made me want to murmur into the coffin my congratulations to Dad for having finished up ahead of the game.

Even the small funerals of the elderly draw enough of a crowd to furnish stabilizing perspectives. I watched Alice through these as she responded to condolences from whitehaired friends and relatives and a half dozen of his now portly and balding former students. I watched her, I imagined, give each of them something precious, as if it were

131

now her office to parcel out Dad's surrendered life like flakes of communion bread. I believed it was the triumph of his luck to have had someone with her poise and assurance with him when he was afraid at the end.

So I was off-balance and unprepared for the chill when she explained to me exactly where he was to be buried. "Beside your mother's grave, of course."

She said it matter-of-factly enough. I was tongue-tied for a moment that threatened to be interminable. I saw how the past had been foreshortened by these ceremonies of burial and, in fact, by his placid years with her. Now it yawned in its full immensity, unfathomable and implacable.

"Is that the way Dad wanted it?"

The graceless question was the best I could manage. Alice redeemed it. "It's the way *we* wanted it," she said. "The way it ought to be."

She would admit no question of fairness to herself. She did not for an instant mean to abdicate her title as his wife. That's who she was and she was giving him back not merely to the earth but to a law as unyielding as mortality. "He ought to be with her," she said, setting her smile and squeezing my hand to help me face it.

Of course she and Dad had made this decision from their common sense intimacy without even thinking to consult us children. They had found no use in stirring up uncertainties in something that could be decided so simply—or that had been decided by circumstances long immune to second thoughts or meddling.

There it was. That is the way the thing was done. After all the discord which none of us living will forget, the man and wife lie in adjacent graves on a cemetery slope close to the farm landscapes of their childhood. I find nothing to add to expand what Alice told me about their full and baffling heritage to us—that it had to be what it was.